Strong Medicine

By BLAKE F. DONALDSON, M.D.

Doubleday & Company, Inc., Garden City, New York, 1962

To my tightly knit and wonderful family:
Mommy and Patty, Sister and Sandy, Johnny
and the Buttercup and Frank

Contents

An Appreciation

Four people have particularly contributed to the publication of this book. Christian A. Johnson found merit in the ideas and exerted his executive ability to get it published in proper form. Through his generosity it will be made available to some of the medical profession specifically interested in internal medicine. The freest possible discussion is desired. Miss Helen Schwartz (or "Salty" as she is more familiarly titled in yachting circles) took time out from her work for Mr. Johnson and from her beloved boat to see that the manuscript was in order.

Miss Clara Claasen is something rare in the publishing world. Prolonged dealing with the mighty in the literary field did not prevent her from finding time to help a struggling amateur. With a ruthless bit of surgery most of the extraneous material in the book was lopped off.

The services of Evelyn Wells were secured in order to insure proper arrangement of the material. As I promptly found out, there is more to arrangement than meets the eye. Mrs. Wells is truly remarkable.

I am tremendously grateful to all of them.

PREFACE

by Charles Gordon Heyd, M.D.

Dr. Donaldson in STRONG MEDICINE expresses his personal concept of treatment for six highly important and frequently deadly diseases—arteriosclerosis, osteoarthritis, heart disease, high blood pressure, diabetes, and gall bladder disease. His book is interesting, informative, humorous, and highly controversial.

This is a book for the laity and the physician. Only a physician with great experience and social responsibility could have written it. The author is a physician dedicated to serving sick people and allaying their disabilities. Of a few of the cases presented in the manuscript I have personal knowledge and have been permitted to observe that they enjoyed a long and better life under his regimen even if they had to make continuous and valiant efforts to obtain it.

There is throughout the text a very definite ethical and philosophical thesis. The author has pleasantly but incisively ranged himself on the side of Ferrero: "It seems to be true of all societies that where pleasure and money are the gods of the multitude, there is a slow but steady weakening of the fibre of character." Certainly his patients who have been successful in increasing their longevity, with amelioration of symptoms, have shown splendid fortitude and developed remarkable inhibitions. They have continued to follow his therapy with a courage and consistency that are truly praiseworthy.

Dr. Donaldson comes from a Scottish ancestry, a race of great people developed under a rather difficult environment but always ready to take up the claymore and fare forth.

He will find many practitioners of medicine willing to accept the challenge and to dispute some or many of his opinions. That in itself is progress, for without critical analysis a doctor would be forever following false leads, leading to no established position in medical practice.

The early antagonism and lack of comprehension on the part of the medical profession concerning the observations of Semmelweis in Vienna and Oliver Wendell Holmes in Boston that childbed or puerperal fever was contagious and the infectious material carried on the hands of the obstetrician or midwife are ample proof that the way of the innovator is indeed hard. In the early days of Listerism—antiseptic surgery —the medical profession confused the philosophy of a new approach to surgical therapy with an attempt to create a new type of chemical treatment for wounds. Samuel D. Gross, "the emperor of American surgery," visited Glasgow in 1868. "Our first stopping place was the old Royal Infirmary, in the building in which Professor Lister first put into practice what is now known as his dressing." The way of the reformer is more difficult than the way of the transgressor. Knowledge comes but wisdom lingers.

The acceptance of any new concept always meets with startling resistance. That in itself is not sufficient to prevent the benefits that may be derived from a different approach to medical therapy and practice. A casual walk—perhaps the doctor's thirty-minute walk before breakfast—will demonstrate that more than half of our population in the third, fourth, or fifth decade of life are overweight or downright obese. Very few of our people exercise or do any real walking. The modern institution of the "coffee break"—coffee and a bun —is certainly responsible for a constantly recurring alimentary intake that must inevitably lead to obesity and its dangerous sequelae.

I have no hesitation in accepting most of the concepts of the author. However, it must be recognized that their successful application to sick people requires an adept psychological approach by the physician, and to many people the regimen may prove on trial unacceptable. It requires great valor to be a dietary hero. Dr. Donaldson's opinions are not haphazard and represent years of observation in a difficult field. Research men and laboratory technicians can well prove or disprove the ideas so plainly and so explicitly expressed throughout his discourse. The fact that his concepts differ from traditional medical practice is bound to produce resistance but for the profession to assume a stationary attitude of mind is to shrivel independent thinking. I can say unequivocally that the regimen prescribed by Dr. Donaldson can be accepted without any danger and in proportion as the directions are carried out the patients will be improved in physical well-being and can be assured that they will live longer in better health and contentment. In addition, the ability of patients to discipline themselves, to carry on the continuous and lifelong habit of abstinence and considered care for their well-being, will certainly provide them with a better mental equipment to live longer in a relatively improved condition of health. Perhaps a great many of our people today are writing their own epitaphs: "Died prematurely from obesity."

The conservation of the individual by medical discipline is indicated in the numerous case reports. Medical treatment is a continuing discipline and there must be a point of sympathy and cheerfulness between the patient and the doctor. The course for the patient is a "tough one."

It is noteworthy that the drawings and portraits depicted by prehistoric man on the walls and roofs of caves in southern France and Spain are composed entirely of edible animals. The men of that period were certainly big and powerful and expended great energy in the search for their animal food.

Medical practice is primarily an intellectual discipline. There was probably no history of medicine prior to Hippocrates, the Greek physician, born about 460 B.C., who has justly been called the Father of Medicine. It was from his teachings that we derived the Hippocratic Oath, now considered one of the most sublime exhortations for the good and simple life, and for the high ethical standards that justly have been associated with the true physician. But, in a larger sense, we owe to Hippocrates three outstanding concepts: accurate observation, careful physical examination, and a codification by means of written records.

In the present volume our interest is aroused constantly by the kindness and patience revealed, and by the observed facts—physical, emotional, and medical. The value of written records is as a basis for personal instruction to the patient. There are no simple injunctions—do this or do that—there is a straightforward time schedule of what the patient should do and, more important, should not do.

Dr. Donaldson has covered in detail and in a discursive

manner most of the outstanding ills that occur in the wide range of medical practice.

Here are exhibited the three primary Christian virtues of faith, hope, and charity, interspersed in many places by an amiable sense of humor.

Chapter I

OLD MAN RIVER

I FIRST became interested in the problem of overweight back in 1919 when I was chief of clinic for Robert Hurtin Halsey, the heart man at the New York Post Graduate Medical School and Hospital. Halsey was the finest teacher I have ever worked for. A cold exterior and a disconcerting habit of asking "Why?" made him hard to know, but once he was satisfied that one of his men was willing to work he would do his level best to try to teach him to think.

The clinic was filled with elderly overweight people who were short of breath. It rapidly became evident that there was a distinct limit to the good that could be accomplished with drugs. Our old standby digitalis made a lot of the arteriosclerotics worse instead of better, and the patients soon became afraid of the shattering effect of drugs that caused a great outpouring of urine.

In many cases obesity was adding too much of a load to failing hearts. It seemed wise to go back to first principles and make a determined effort to get rid of the smothering fat.

Even in those days we thought there was nothing to the treatment of obesity but to see that patients exactly adhered to a low-calorie diet. If the output of energy exceeded the intake, weight loss had to be automatic. It was not realized that low-calorie diets mean relative starvation with attendant weakness and hunger. Patients can't work when they feel weak and steal food when they are hungry. And if there is any lesson that a physician, exposed to the teeming millions in New York's lower east side, learns it is that people must be kept on their feet and working at something.

At the end of a year a brief survey of clinic patients on low-calorie diets showed that the results were something worse than terrible. And they were no better in my office practice.

It was understandable perhaps in clinic work. Dispensary patients may be born failures with a tendency to fail at everything. But if more intelligent patients in the office were unable to lose weight successfully there had to be something wrong with the method.

Of the forty-eight years since I graduated from medical school, the twenty-seven most rewarding were spent in the wards and at the autopsy tables of the old New York City Hospital on Blackwell's Island. There I saw the evil terminal effects of obesity and there the words "obesity sextette" came into use by the profession.

Fat seems to predispose to six killers in medicine. Heart disease, diabetes, arteriosclerosis, high blood pressure, osteo-arthritis and gallstones can, and do, occur in thin people, but in a vast majority overweight seems to precipitate the trouble. And any correct treatment involves a return to normal weight.

There are exceedingly few medical men who are entitled

to call themselves specialists in any one of the obesity sextette. The word "specialist" implies a comprehensive knowledge of the most effective treatment: the ability to routinely remove three pounds of fat a week from co-operative patients, until such time as the body weight is normal. Then a change has to be made so that weight stays at a correct level. In a busy practice such a technique can result in the elimination of three to four thousand pounds of excess weight a year, and not the miserable average amount of forty or fifty pounds from all of the patients put together. A lot more interest needs to be shown, and a lot more work needs to be done.

It has been my observation that even in the most modern and best equipped of clinics the results of antiobesity treatment are poor. Some of the large clinics fail to take off *and keep off* more than ninety pounds of fat a year from all of their patients put together, whereas a need may exist to remove five thousand pounds of excess fat from the cardiacs.

Not long ago I had the privilege of inspecting a big cardiac clinic. The chief of clinic showed me a whole museum of twisted heart valves, unusual electrocardiograms, and the records of surgical results in birth defects.

"How have the patients been most benefited in the last year?" I asked.

The chief went on the defensive immediately and wanted to know what I meant by the question.

So I told him. "Useful surgery for the heart will probably always be an exceedingly limited field. Enthusiastic surgeons often fail to realize that when valves are badly damaged the heart muscle may be in even worse shape. Birth defects in the heart can be associated with other physical and mental irregularities in the body and have a big inherited factor. Oftentimes it is unwise to try to upset the balance of nature. She knows what she is doing, and in the long run it can be better for the patient to get along with what comes naturally.

"Then too, just as in tuberculosis today, the rheumatic infections that used to cripple so many hearts seem to be on the way out. The real future in heart work is to get rid of the obesity that may predispose to arteriosclerotic heart disease.

"How many pounds of fat have you taken off and kept off the overweight patients in your clinic this year? To me that seems the best measure of a clinic's efficiency."

He was nonplused. Apparently the idea had never occurred to him even though the treatment of obesity should have been his main weapon in prevention and treatment.

Strength lies in simplicity and the new medical treatment of the obese is simple and strong. Wide application of the method is needed. For the sun is coming up at long last for the obese. We have learned how to reduce weight without weakness or hunger, and that is a great advance. How it all came about is interesting, and I used to delight in demonstrating the new technique to the internes at the New York City Hospital during grand rounds.

I wish I could recapture in print the spirit of some of the Saturday mornings.

My staff, along with some guest famous for a particular line of medical endeavor, would show up at eight o'clock Saturday morning at my home. Essie Sherman, a marvelous cook and an old family retainer, would stage one of her scrumptious breakfasts, after which we trooped off to the hospital conference room on Blackwell's Island. The interne staff would be waiting in amphitheater walls hallowed by the clinics of the great Edward Janeway and Harlow Brooks and Evan Evans. Interesting cases of the week and anything else pertaining to medicine would come under open discussion.

The pathologist might demonstrate that our thinking was right, or half right, or all wrong.

Hospital work in medicine often tends to deal with bizarre manifestations of the worn-out dying, while office practice is more concerned with the careless living. The primary goal is to turn out internes who are well-rounded physicians, for the stars are there if you can just teach them to look up. Office practice is often neglected in interne training, so it was my custom at times to bring over to the hospital groups of patients who were suffering from certain disorders and who had been under continued observation in the office for ten to twenty years. The patients seemed to enjoy the experience and it was certain that the internes did. Endlessly they would quiz patients with something like a blood pressure of 230/110 as to whether they really had lost fifty pounds in weight and walked thirty minutes every morning, and eaten a lot of fat meat three times a day, and were still working. Such sessions constitute good teaching.

But it is a bygone era I have been describing. There seems to be no time available nowadays to savor the full joys of medicine.

Some of my old Post Graduate students still make regular pilgrimages from Africa or Australia or some other remote spot. They seem to like to put on white coats and work with me in the office for a few days. Regular human question marks they are, and the opening gun is almost always, "What's new in medicine?" Many of them seem to think the problems in a place like Pretoria differ little from those on Park Avenue. Often I've wanted to go and see how they apply the new ideas that I have tried to demonstrate.

When they leave, it is always with the same old question: "When are you going to put this down in black and white?"

The internes used to listen in wonder when I told them

that in my opinion office practice roughly resolves into the treatment of obesity and its complications in thirty per cent of the cases, and that sixty-five per cent of the patients complain of allergic manifestations. In other words, about three people out of ten are too fat and two out of every three have allergy.

That leaves only five per cent for the rest of medicine.

Of course, if the new theory is sound, the emphasis in medical teaching should be changed, along with the eating and shopping habits of the nation. Any book that is written about the simple aspects of medicine should concern itself with the mental processes of the little woman pushing a cart through the country's shopping centers. What she buys, or doesn't buy, can make manufacturers tremble and governments totter. In her hands lies the health of the nation. When she uses bad judgment in the kitchen the results are manifest in the office.

The physician has a triple problem in outlining treatment for the ordinary troubles of life.

First of all, the patients need to have some inherited ability to exactly follow orders.

Then a good way of life has to be prescribed in words that are clearly understood.

Lastly, having given the orders, the physician still has to do ninety per cent of the work. He has to see that the orders are carried out. A valiant effort must be made to correct the symptoms that can be corrected, and to check up regularly on patients to see that they continue to live well. In spite of all his efforts, at least twenty-five per cent of his patients can be expected to fall by the wayside.

But the other wonderful seventy-five per cent, who can and do follow orders, are their own and the physician's reward. What the doctor has learned they try to apply, and they take the ups and downs of life with trust and courage. Such patients make one humble and realize what an inestimable privilege it is to be a physician.

As for the failing twenty-five per cent, they give up because the prescription of simple living is medicine too strong for them to take. What they really want is to buy some miracle drug that will enable them to live in carefree fashion. But nature does not stoop to miracles.

In my office, as in every medical office, miracle drugs flood the mails. The secretary deals with them by dropping them into the wastebasket, so that I shall not be bothered. Time, and bitter experience, have made me completely skeptical of something one gets for nothing. Only a tiny fraction of these free drug samples have any real value.

The give-away vitamins, hormones, drugs to wake up by, go to sleep by, not to worry by, prevent blood clotting, prevent anemia, cure constipation, and aid weight loss—all are pretty much in the wishful-thinking class and usually do far more harm than good.

As the years roll by I find myself resorting less and less to drugs in the effort to combat disease processes. We can still practice about all the medicine that is worth while with six standard drugs, plus a few new ones. The place to investigate new drugs is in a hospital where controls are available. A doctor's office is not an experimental station and patients should resent being fitted to a sample drug, even if it is "for free."

For some years I've been under pressure to get my ideas of what is worth while in living written down in a way that both doctors and patients—and the little lady with the grocery list—can read with pleasure and perhaps profit.

A cold Sunday in January, in the middle of Long Island,

seems a queer time and place to be bitten by the demon ambition to write about medicine.

With wild cherry log flames roaring up the chimney of the Franklin stove, drowsing over the new seed catalogue is the order of the day. Life, which heretofore has gone by for me at headlong pace, has reached a stage quite like Indian summer. With most of the harvest in, a pleasant haze lies just over the horizon, and while the telephone is blessedly silent there is nothing to do but to recharge my batteries.

Then the seed catalogue injects a sour note with a picture of those new and supposedly desirable "nearest to white" marigolds. I dislike marigolds in my garden. Even the ordinary kind attract too many Japanese beetles, and the whiter they are the more beetles. Why, I find myself wondering, does a penalty always seem to attach to anything that is new?

It occurs to me that in medicine we have a great many things comparable to "nearest to white" marigolds. Really important things have the strength of simplicity, and I find myself considering what I have done in my own lifetime to simplify medicine.

Thousands of patients come to memory, offering their mute testimony to work done over the years.

The only possible contribution I can make to human knowledge is to put on record my own clinical impressions of human disease and carelessness in living. Clinical impressions do not constitute scientific proof, even though they have often been the forerunners of great advances in medicine. Only time, and the work of great research men in many lands, can establish anything as the scientific truth.

But the ideas demonstrated at the old City Hospital grand rounds have apparently stood the test of time and I offer them here simply for what they are worth.

In this book repetition will be evident but that is intentional. In any medical teaching it seems desirable to make a point three times in order to drive it home.

Quite early I developed the practice of writing out explicit orders, designed to emphasize the new ideas for controlling obesity, for patients to follow. Verbal orders often fail to register because many people lack the ability to concentrate. Also, the new ideas in weight losing are not generally accepted yet. They are too radical and too new.

And many overweight people are emotional. The doctor is not running a debating society. Never give an emotional patient a choice. If permitted his choice of two things the emotional patient will take four. Written down in black and white he has orders he cannot easily ignore.

Fast weight reduction with two items for each meal is more readily accomplished by emotional people than is slow reduction with three things for each meal.

So orders must be like the treatment itself—simple and strong and expressed in the clearest terms.

Doubts assail me.

Medicine has in it all the drama of life and death, wonder and awe and majesty, pathos and stark staring tragedy, humor and low comedy. One would need the gift of tongues and of angels to describe it. And literary skill requires an inherited bent with endless practice in making words sing. None of these do I have, so that would suggest the need of a competent ghost writer. Negative! Medicine has too much dignity to allow for the liberties a ghost writer might take. Booth Tarkington was right when he said that as a man gets along in years the respect of his colleagues becomes all important. And one should stand or fall by his own written word.

There are other qualms. If a book does not have a certain

literary value it won't be published. Publishers are not in business for their health.

Still the contentious new ideas might carry a book, if complicated medical terminology could be avoided.

When opportunities have been great in medicine some sort of an accounting of stewardship is in order. It isn't right to have so much of what you think you have learned die with you.

Practicing medicine in a great and wonderful city for forty-eight years puts one a little in the class of Old Man River. You must know something, if you just keep rolling along.

Discarding the seed catalogue, I resolutely turn to my desk, with a cheerful thought paraphrasing Admiral Farragut: "Damn the split infinitives! Go ahead!"

Chapter II

GETTING STARTED

I DON'T KNOW of any better way to get interested in the study of medicine than to be obliged to weed long rows of onions on a hot day, especially when one is a little boy eleven years old. Weeding onions allows plenty of time to decide what else you would rather do.

A bit of bad luck had banished me to this no man's land.

I had been playing checkers, seated on a pile of horse blankets at the rear of the store, with one of the loafers who hung around the place. It was a pastime that was permitted only as long as I won. My father had no use for a loser. A careless move cost me the game and Father his temper. I was promptly hurled into the outer darkness of the garden with orders to clear the onion rows.

In those days every activity was important. What was eaten in the wintertime depended on successful farming during the summer.

Both of my grandfathers, strong-minded men of Scottish descent, firmly believed that "Satan finds mischief for idle hands to do." Hunting and fishing and baseball were only approved of after the work was done. And my two older brothers and I were given plenty of it.

It is of course our grandparents who make us tick. More than any other factor in life they color our way of thinking. Parents are merely the carriers of traits.

In the practice of medicine a doctor considers himself fortunate if he has a patient who can give an account of his four grandparents. They give a clear picture of the patient and what he can expect by way of a healthy and successful life.

I've never taken time out before to think of our family background, but they must have been rather remarkable people.

The store had been built by Grandpa Wallace Donaldson. He was born in a house on the Bowery at a time when that district was noted for flowers rather than flophouses, and had been launched early in life by his Glasgow-born father into the business of wholesale packing and distribution of meat. Irritated by a worthless partner, in time Grandpa sold the business, loaded his family and household goods onto a barge, and in tow of a sailboat started up Long Island Sound. He had no particular destination in mind. Sailing up the Nissequogue River, they found the gnats and mosquitoes intolerable. Grandpa heard of a crossroads in the center of Long Island where insect pests were not a problem. Ox teams were hired and the family possessions were carted over to the little village of Hauppauge, an Indian name meaning sweet water.

I still live there.

At Hauppauge, Grandpa Donaldson established a trading post and country store, along with a big three-story home. There my father, and in time my brothers and I, spent happy, healthy, and hard-working boyhoods. Grandpa Donaldson was the kindest man I have ever known. There were always shotgun shells and fishing tackle to be had for our asking in the store.

After his retirement it was the "sea room" offered by the Sound that had brought my other grandfather, John Scott, and his family to Long Island and the nearby hamlet of St. James. Grandfather Scott, whose family hailed from Edinburgh, led an adventurous life; at the age of eleven he had run away to sea. By the time he was twenty-two he was commanding his own ship.

Those were the days of the great clippers in the China tea trade and Grandfather was a sea captain in the best tradition of iron men in wooden ships. The picture of one of his ships, the *N. B. Palmer*, hangs on the wall of my dining room today. When she docked at South Ferry, gleaming in black and vermilion paint, the New York gentry were honored to be invited to dine in the ship's cabin with Captain Scott and his family.

Several of Grandfather Scott's five children were born at sea. My mother had gone around the world twice in sail, and could describe to us her fearful recollections of the storms rounding Cape Horn.

In a sense, all the members of those past generations were cast in the role of pioneers. Indeed the old folks seemed to have had one quality in common: they lacked any fear of the unknown.

The medical histories of these two families show the advances made by science within the past century. At that time children came to adulthood, it was believed, only by the grace of God. Parents expected to lose many of their brood to death. Of Grandfather Scott's five children, only one was a boy. The lad was the pride of his life and his inseparable companion.

Today scarlet fever is not regarded as a killer, but it hit this little boy at a time when doctors thought it inadvisable to give water to a patient with a high fever. In his delirium the boy kept calling to his father for "a drink, Daddy." But the father dared not go against medical orders, and the boy died with that plaintive cry ringing in my grandfather's ears.

On the other side of the family, over at Hauppauge, seven children were born to my Donaldson grandparents and only one survived. He was to be my father.

What were the killers then?

Grandpa kept the finest of Jersey cows to provide milk for his family. The cream was lowered in a pail down the well to keep it cool. I hate to think of the processes that went on in that delicacy before it reached the table. Summer diarrhea with its attendant sun cholera mixture were regarded as normal events in a child's life. Scarlet fever, diphtheria, and tuberculosis ran unchecked through families.

The race was to the swift and only the strongest survived.

My father, William Wallace Donaldson, made it. By the time he was seven he was carrying the mail on foot from Hauppauge to the old Suffolk railroad station, three miles away. At eleven he started going to New York twice a week to buy goods for the store. Later he took over the post office and bookkeeping. Gradually he assumed the drawing up of wills and deeding property and small village banking.

Little formal education was available, even if there had been time for it in his busy life, but nothing ever shook him from his daily habit of spending one hour a day with his beloved New York Herald. He was a well-informed man with many friends.

Time out was found for courting. Grandfather staked him to the fastest horse on Long Island, along with a good Stuyver's runabout. With these assets it wasn't too difficult to capture the interest of Nellie Scott, the oldest daughter of the retired sea captain over in St. James. She married Father to settle down in Hauppauge and become known to us in time as "the little Mither."

We boys helped out in the store, and I soon learned there was one order I could fill better than either Grandpa or Father. In those days country stores dispensed quite a variety of simple drugs. When cough medicine was demanded, it was the custom to take a bottle of syrup of squill, a bottle of sweet spirits of niter, and a bottle of paregoric, and mix all these together. The natives liked my prescription best. That was probably because I doubled up on the paregoric. It stopped their coughing and everything else, I suppose.

In her gentle way our little Mither had a will of iron. She held to the old Scottish tradition that one of her boys should be either a minister or a doctor or a lawyer. For some reason she had me headed early for the ministry, which brings me back to the middle of the onion patch on that hot afternoon when I was eleven years old. I found myself considering a remark Mither had made the evening before.

One of my two beagle pups had begun to howl piteously and Mither and I had gone downstairs to see what was wrong. We found him coughing up blood in agony. We quieted his struggles by wrapping him in a blanket. Mither pried open his jaws.

By the light of the kitchen lamp I was able to look down the dog's throat. Deep down, the light glinted on the exposed portion of a darning needle stuck crosswise in the base of the poor beast's tongue. Only an inch of the steel was visible.

With two pliers and a bit of luck I was able to break the needle in the middle and drag out both ends.

While the pup was gratefully lapping water and Mither

and I were washing our hands, she spoke, carefully choosing her words.

"Laddie," she said, "I've been watching you, and I've been thinking that you'll never have the makings of a minister. So we might try for you to be a doctor."

It seemed like a good idea.

So my future was settled that hot afternoon in the onion patch, and at the age of seventeen I matriculated at the Long Island College Hospital in Brooklyn.

When I was in my freshman year Dr. John Osborne Polak, the director of the obstetric and gynecology division of the hospital, suggested that I assist in the outpatient department.

Seventeen is a little young to be helping bring babies into the world, but life itself was regarded as a liberal education in those days, and it still is.

Dr. Polak was one of the great men of his era and he will long be remembered, even if he did fail eventually to make an obstetrician of me. Over and over he emphasized in his teaching that we students were not supposed to be obstetricians as yet, but just good midwives. Aseptic expectancy was his motto, and his insistence upon germproof cleanliness under some of the conditions we met with seemed at times an impossibly high standard.

I recall a house visit out on Livonia Avenue in East New York when I found myself in real trouble. As usual, no nurse was available, and the student in attendance on the mother was worn out by watching her case of delayed labor. I sent him home and took over myself. Only one sterile outfit was available in my bag but the woman had been examined regularly in the antepartum clinic at the hospital and pronounced normal. No particular difficulty was to be expected.

The baby finally arrived and while I was working over it I experienced a curious sensation. My shoes were sticking to the

floor. Blood was soaking through the mattress. A hasty examination showed that the woman was bleeding like a fire
hydrant and that there was another baby inside still to come.

A partially separated placenta with severe hemorrhage con-
stitutes one of the great obstetric emergencies. The woman's
face was ashy gray and she had the air hunger that goes
with tremendous blood loss. My sterile equipment was used
up. If the loss was great enough we had been taught to pack
with anything at hand, including even the comforter on the
bed. But that was bad, too, because subsequent infection
would often be fatal.

One more look at the woman and I dashed for the hall,
where the husband, sensing disaster, was sitting under the
wall telephone vomiting down the steps. With that obstacle
removed I got Polak on the line. That great man was always
on the job in case one of his youngsters was in trouble.

"Steady, boy," he said. "Now go over that again. . . . Can
she make the hospital?"

"Yes, sir," I gulped.

"There will be an ambulance there in twenty minutes. Do
whatever you think best."

That could well have been the longest twenty minutes of
my life, while the woman's lifeblood continued to drain away.

Rumor had spread through the neighborhood that the
young medical student had killed the woman. When we got
the stretcher out on the street the ambulance was surrounded
with angry upturned faces and shaking fists. But the police
took care of the situation and at the hospital Polak was waiting to do his usual splendid job.

A week later the woman went back to Livonia Avenue with
a healthy pair of twins.

And I had learned that the infallible way to diagnose twins
is to count them as they come out.

In the year 1913 when I was just inside the law that made twenty-one a requisite for practicing medicine, the New York Board of Regents certified that I was qualified. I made it with four weeks to spare. Dr. Polak was doing a lot of research on twilight sleep at the time and he offered me a chance to go on with him. It was a temptation to learn obstetrics under a great teacher, but I had never cared much for mechanical work. I had a hankering to try my wings at internal medicine.

That chance came when one of the great charity hospitals in the world opened its doors to me.

The old New York City Hospital had some brilliant men on its staff. Among them were Nathaniel Potter, who had translated Sahli's *Diagnostic Methods*; C. N. B. Camac, who had been trained by Sir William Osler; Evan Evans, with the finest medical mind of his time; Harlow Brooks, the widely beloved physician; and Robert Cooke, who had done the first scientific work on asthma and hay fever. All of them would skip their practices in the middle of the morning to journey over to Blackwell's Island and watch John Larkin do his stuff. He was perhaps the most experienced gross pathologist of all time, and with masterly skill would demonstrate the cause of some hotly debated and obscure death.

Having passed the examination for internship at City Hospital, I went on duty there with a year as pathological interne under Larkin preceding the regular service. The chief knew so much, and was so patient in trying to impart his knowledge, that it was no sacrifice on my part to become his willing slave. All over town I trailed him in his autopsy work. Besides our own work at the Russell Sage laboratory, we covered the City Home, the Metropolitan, the City Morgue at Bellevue, and Quarantine on Swinburne Island.

During my regular internship I fell under the spell of the great men whose names I have already mentioned, and of

John Fordyce, the skin man. He always had a pocketful of
fine cigars for his internes. That amiable habit is neglected
now by visiting physicians. If I had an interneship to do
over again I would spend far more time in the skin wards
and the X-ray interpretation room. They are both basic
sciences in internal medicine, and it is impossible to know
enough about them.

Harlow Brooks used to arrive promptly at seven o'clock in
the morning to make rounds. Attendance of the full staff
was optional at that time in the morning and usually I had
that wonderful man and great teacher all to myself. Indeed
all of the visiting physicians tried to impart to us striplings
that curious intangible something called "diagnostic flair."
That is the ability, based on powers of observation cultivated
by years of experience, to quickly spot what is wrong with a
patient.

I saw Evan Evans do this once. I was his houseman. He
liked to come over to the island on the two o'clock boat and
teach from two well-worked-up cases. A house physician who
was on his job would arrange such a setup.

At eleven o'clock one morning a new patient was admitted
to my wards. Examination showed that it was probable that
he had been eating "measly" pork. He was a German who
liked to eat raw hamburger steak. If the grinder had been used
in making sausage before the beef was ground, and the pork
was infected, the portal of entry was obvious. The worms
from infected pork are usually killed by freezing, and as most
pork is frozen nowadays not so much of the disease is seen.
But in the old days it was not too uncommon. The worms in
"measly" pork burrow through the intestine and can invade
all tissues in the body, including the heart and spinal cord.
Inasmuch as it was eleven o'clock in the morning I hurried to

the laboratory and persuaded the pathologist and bacteriologist to postpone their luncheon hour. The staff was concentrated on the problem and we went to work. A blood count was made to look for the white blood cells characteristic of the disease. Spinal fluid was removed and centrifuged for worms. A piece of muscle was removed from the biceps for examination, and a plate taken of the heart, from a distance of six feet, to look for any enlargement that might suggest invasion of the heart muscle. (If a target such as the heart is too close to the X-ray machine the image will seem enlarged.) Three microscopes were set up beside the patient's bed with slides of the blood, the muscle, and the spinal fluid.

When Evans came into the big sixty-bed ward at two o'clock we were lined up waiting for him. Fifty feet away across the ward the new patient was sitting up in bed grasping his arm with an expression of pain. A beam of sunshine striking his head showed up the telltale ring of swelling above the eyes that is characteristic of the disease.

Without breaking stride Evans grasped my arm and asked, "Good Lord, boy, when did you admit the case of trichiniasis?"

A small incident, perhaps, but it took a brain that functioned like a Rolls-Royce engine. I've always felt that there really were giants in those days.

When my interneship was over I transferred my belongings to the New York Post Graduate Medical School and Hospital, where one of the attending doctors, Robert Cooke, had secured for me the post of resident physician. The salary of one hundred dollars a month seemed to me a princely sum, and at long last I was on my own.

After nine months I was sent on active duty to the Mexican border as a lieutenant in the old Medical Reserve Corps.

Back in New York I received a captain's commission and enlisted the personnel of Base Hospital No. Eight. We were assigned to the second convoy leaving for France on our way to World War I.

Chapter III

C'EST LA GUERRE

I DON'T INTEND to dwell on the experience overseas. It cured me of ever again seeing any glamor in war, but in several unexpected ways it left me with food for thought.

At the base hospital in Savenay I was given charge of the tuberculosis camp. There I encountered a lot of what was apparently acute lower lobe tuberculosis. That is a fairly rare condition, but as confirmation we had good fluoroscopic examinations and a well-run laboratory.

Lacking transportation for these cases back to the States because the ships had to turn around as soon as they were unloaded, all I could do in treatment was to insure perfect bed rest. Nature heals tuberculosis by surrounding the affected areas with delicate scar tissue. Any physical effort sends this scar tissue flying. It rapidly became evident that armed guards were a necessity to insure complete bed rest. Permission for this was secured. No patient was allowed toilet privileges. Four months later space was available to send the patients back home. There a board of experts cast doubt on the diagnosis of tuberculosis. The X rays were clear. The men seemed well and were ordered back to duty in France. By that time a real tuberculosis expert, Gerald Webb of Colorado Springs, had come to the hospital to assume charge. I met Webb later and he told me that I would be interested to learn that every single man of the group that had been sent back to France had broken down again with open tuberculosis.

I still believe that the best treatment for early soft tuberculosis is to stay in bed for ninety days, without getting up to pass urine or anything else.

One morning I was told to report to the commanding officer. He was in a bad mood after a reprimand from headquarters about eight men in the psychiatric wards who had managed to commit suicide. In studying my record he found that I had done some research work on paresis. He said he was "damn sick of psychiatrists who let men commit suicide, and sent back to duty men who took pot shots at their lieutenants." I was to take over and use some common sense.

I had the temerity to say that I didn't know the foggiest thing about psychiatry. All the comfort I got out of this was, "It's an order."

Shades of John Larkin! Me a nut picker! It just goes to show you what the Army can do to a man. But I followed orders and tried common sense and what I learned proved of value later in treating emotional patients.

It seemed to me that it would help prevent brooding if the patients got out of doors and took some form of exercise.

So every morning the two hundred or so shell-shock cases were sent out to march with full equipment. Some would turn white and keel over in the road and others would turn various colors and pass out. But I kept them going. When the last of them were in trouble I would reverse the march and pick up the stragglers. It was always a terrible-looking outfit that finally got back to the hospital gate. The commanding officer would be out praying that some inspector would not come along. But I got ninety per cent of them back to duty at some other kind of work than action with combat troops. That was a lot better than letting them become lifelong Veterans' Bureau addicts.

I had profited more than I knew by the experience. I had learned that many of the troubles in life can be walked off.

Then orders came to proceed to Paris. I was to command the gas hospital, Red Cross Military Hospital No. Six at Bellevue, halfway out to Versailles from the Montparnasse Station.

We took over just as the Boche began using chlorine and phosgene and mustard gas. Eventually the use of mustard gas predominated because a wounded soldier is more of a handicap to an army than a dead one. The burned men were floated down the Seine River on barges and then transferred to the hospital, arriving in lots of one and two hundred.

By much overcrowding and with the addition of some tents pitched on the grounds we were able to set up seven hundred beds. Work began to flood in and as commanding officer I had some headaches. I had to be my own adjutant, and medical director, and ward surgeon for two hundred and sixty of the seven hundred patients.

At first the hospital wards were a moaning horror, for the pain of mustard gas burns can be dreadful. Then we learned the trick of taking the tops off jam jars and melting the paraffin to spray on the burned skin. It seemed to give instant relief and to check infection.

The main dining hall had been converted into a ward of sixty beds for the most serious cases. When lips are burned with mustard gas it means that a great deal of gas has been inhaled. Gradually a cast would form over the windpipe and main bronchi. The cast would look like an inverted eelskin.

Somewhere between the nineteenth and twenty-first days after gas had been inhaled, the cast would break loose and the patient would suffocate in a horrible manner. Treatment availed nothing. The worst of it was that the boys with badly burned lips all knew what was in store for them.

One day a fine Hungarian violinist came through to play for the wounded. As he climbed to the musicians' gallery overlooking the hall, he told me he would like to have the men ask for selections they might like to hear. Never have I heard anyone with so extensive a musical repertoire.

A young Southern boy was lying on a cot in the middle of the ward. His lips were burned almost off. He was on his eighteenth day. He beckoned to me, and when I went over to him he whispered: "Sir, would you ask the man if he can play the '*Missouri* Waltz?'"

As the strains of that old melody swept through the hall I had to leave. Some things in life you just can't take.

Before taking charge of the gas hospital, I was no different from most Americans in military service. I had often entertained the idea that some of my commanding officers were slightly out of their minds. But when you get a crack at command yourself things seem a lot different. I learned something that stood me in good stead in later years. Only a dozen or so of the one hundred and fifty in personnel could exactly follow out an order. The others would change the order a little or a lot. In the Army, failure to follow out an order can lead to court-martial. There was no time for such nonsense and I learned to give suggestions rather than orders. It seems to me that that percentage of people unable to carry out exact orders holds true in civil life, and one must be tolerant.

Probably the most constructive idea I got out of my military service developed from the observation of patients in the shell-shock wards at Savenay. A great problem, of course, in the military service is what happens under the stress of combat.

In the First and Second World Wars and then, according to reports, in the Korean War, one third of the men would fail to shoot their weapons when attacked. Under imminent peril to their lives, they would freeze up. It did not matter how much training they had received in the skillful employment of their weapons. The condition is, of course, a reaction to what is felt to be an impossible situation. It is not a matter of cowardice. Any good soldier with common sense constantly suffers some fear during an attack. Under the appalling conditions of modern warfare, with the terror at night of perimeter defense, two out of three will defend their lives and try to take any reasonable objectives ordered, and one out of three will not.

As a medical officer I often found myself obliged to attend court-martials. It was tough to see boys ordered shot for not carrying out duties you knew were impossible for them. They should never have been placed in positions where they had to fail.

When a medical officer is assigned as counsel for the defense at a military court-martial, he is quite up against it in his own mind if the defendant has been caught in the act of shooting off his own toe or finger. The counsel for the defense may have examined the unfortunate soldier and obtained a history of one or two grandparents who were drunkards or who had violent tempers. Then on physical examination he may have noted that the defendant had huge pupils, one third of an inch separation between two front incisor teeth, and a depression in his breastbone in which you could put half a grapefruit. While the soldier was being examined, sweat was pouring from his armpits and his heart was racing.

The problem was then, and still is, how to convince the

hard-boiled line officers composing the court that the fault lay with the doctor who enlisted a man who could always be expected to do the wrong thing under combat conditions. It is a nice problem in ethics and in common sense.

Can the thirty-three per cent who react to combat in this unfortunate way be spotted in advance of prolonged and expensive training?

I think they can.

It could be accomplished by a good physical examination. It seemed to me that about ninety-nine per cent of the men in the shell-shock wards had many of the physical irregularities called stigmata of degeneracy. The human animal, of course, has a mixed-up background. There aren't any of us who haven't got ancestors somewhere in the dim past who were horse thieves, people with violent tempers, or people with physical defects. Such traits can be expected to show up now and then.

The main physical signs that are looked for on examination are:

1. Irregularly shaped bodies.
2. Big pupils and marked early vision defects.
3. Perforated nasal septa.
4. Extremely irregular dentition with or without widely separated front teeth.
5. Caved-in breastbones.
6. Long fingers with blue hands.
7. Profuse sweating during the course of a physical examination.
8. The finding of an exceedingly strong anal sphincter muscle which makes rectal examination difficult and painful.
9. Developmental defects like ruptures and pilonidal cysts.
10. Exceptionally fast heart rates.
11. Color combinations after the second generation.

The war did come to an end. Preferring not to sit around in the mud awaiting transportation home, I applied for duty with the Army of Occupation. Two days after the armistice my orders came to join Evacuation Hospital No. Four in charge of the medical service. The hospital was established in Coblenz when influenza began to take its terrible toll among the exhausted, poorly shod, and insufficiently clad troops who had marched into Germany. The hospital wards were swamped with them. The convalescent patients helped out in the wards as soon as they could stagger around. In spite of our efforts, on one terrible day eighteen patients died.

Even today there is no specific treatment for real epidemic influenza. You wouldn't have to raise the virulence of epidemic influenza a great deal to have a practical version of Gabriel's trumpet.

Whenever it is around, exhaustion and chilling are to be avoided at all costs.

I was the only one of the officers who hadn't had a leave during the war and was given a chance to go to Scotland, the land I had most wanted to visit. But word came that a transport would be available to take us home. At that stage of the game, if necessary, I think I would have come home on a raft.

Discharged at last, it was good to find the folks awaiting me at the railroad station in Smithtown. Father was pleased that I'd gotten a majority out of it, and Mither and our faithful maid Hannah Titus wept for the mince pies they had sent me and which the too vigilant post office inspectors had searched for bombs.

I had planned to stay home a couple of months, but after three days I couldn't stand being idle. I had to get into New York to find out how I was going to make a living. By dint of depositing alternate Army pay checks in a bank in New York, seventeen hundred dollars had been saved up.

One thing more—while I needed it and could have used it many times, I never applied for the bonus Congress voted. For me it would have amounted to about fifteen hundred dollars, but there was something about it that held me back. I had seen many better men than I could ever hope to be die without a bonus. Taking that money seemed to be letting them down.

In this world a man should stand on his own two unaided feet.

Chapter IV

LAUNCHED INTO PRACTICE

IT WAS 1919, and other medical men were returning from service. Among them was the famous heart man Robert Halsey, just back from overseas. He wanted someone to rent his office in the afternoon and work as chief of his cardiac clinic at the New York Post Graduate Medical School and Hospital, and offered me the chance. I didn't hesitate. The Army had shown me that I needed to know a lot more about a basic branch of internal medicine, that of the heart.

So after renting a hall bedroom on New York's east side, with each leg of the bed in a can of kerosene to keep off the crimson ramblers, I was all set.

Robert Halsey in New York and Paul White in Boston and Thomas Lewis and James MacKenzie in England were the great pioneers in the field of cardiology. Halsey was that rare combination, a pure scientist and a splendid clinician.

During his time in military service he had been mulling over an idea that it might be worth while to give school children with crippled rheumatic hearts special opportunities to

survive the rigors of childhood. So, with the enthusiastic co-
operation of the New York Board of Health and the Board
of Education, we tackled the problem. A ground-floor school
down on Avenue A was assigned to us. Out of some seventy
thousand school children in that district the New York Board
of Health physicians had picked out six hundred cardiacs.
Under Halsey's close personal supervision we threw out, as
not having heart disease at all, all but two hundred and
twenty. The rest simply had accidental murmurs, or fast heart
rates, or blue hands, or irregular rhythms, and really had
nothing wrong with their hearts. They represented quite a
serious error because it takes a long time to disabuse the mind
of a child and his parents of the idea that there is something
wrong with the motor. Also the error in diagnosing these children probably explained the medical reports in circulation at
the time of rheumatic heart disease cured by tonsillectomy.
Such children never had heart disease to begin with, and as
their chests expanded with age the accidental murmurs disappeared. Tonsillectomy in rheumatic heart disease is just as
much indicated as it ever was, but it is done more to prevent additional infection.

Tonsils were removed, elaborate dental care arranged for,
and supplemental feeding provided. Then I did the necessary
leg work, which consisted of going to the home of every child
who failed to show up for school. Nursing care was provided
and an effort was made to carry them through infections.
Long flights of tenement stairs can be wearisome but the re-
wards in medicine are great. Once the grandmothers were
convinced that we were in earnest in our desire to help, nothing was too good for the "Professor." I'd be invited to special
dinners of *gebratener Kalbfleisch* or *gefüllter fisch*, when I
would have an opportunity to enhance my Jewish vocabulary.
And the warmhearted Italian people always had a relative

who ran a restaurant. They would put on a real dinner party with baby octopus cooked in garlic and oil and everything else. Poor folk make loyal patients. At the time of the great financial depression wealthy patients stayed away in droves, but the poor stuck with me. And at a time when I desperately needed moral support, at my wedding in St. Thomas' Church, the whole school for cardiacs attended in a body to back me up and cheer my lovely bride. Good youngsters, all of them, and a few are still going strong.

But it became evident after a time that children with badly damaged hearts are too great a risk to make it worth while to provide a special public school for them. Some of the work we started, however, is still going on in private institutions.

By this time I had completed a year of futile endeavor in trying to get the fat cardiacs in the clinic to lose weight on low-calorie diets.

Halsey had taught me a couple of basic facts: that almost nothing is known about what is normal; and that all cells in the human body have qualities in common and then specialize afterward.

It might be that the cells had common needs in nutrition. The best food to prevent cataracts in the eyes and holes in the teeth might be the same food that would best prevent and treat migraine and duodenal ulcer and heart disease.

The teeth are always the easiest system in the human body to study. They can be directly inspected and dental caries exactly followed by X ray. The idea occurred to me that if the best food to prevent dental caries could be found it might be the best food to prevent everything else, including obesity. Obviously any food used to prevent dental caries and obesity must be normal to begin with. But what in the world is normal?

All over the globe eating habits vary depending upon the

availability of food. The Mongolian peoples get along on rice and soybeans. Northern Africans dote on a combination of flour and hot peppers that seems frequently to cause gastric ulcers. Northern Italians may eat polenta (corn meal mush) three times a day. In the deep South collards and sow belly are still high in public esteem. The swollen bellies of children in Central America depend upon bananas. But all of the more primitive peoples seem to crave fat if they can get it. In Central Africa natives will paddle long distances to get at the fat-yielding body of a dead hippopotamus.

It so happens that in this country all kinds of foods are in plentiful supply. My problem then was what to choose among them in the effort to establish the normal.

It is always well to begin at the beginning, so I paid a visit to the American Museum of Natural History to see what teeth were like in the dawn of history.

Those assistant curators in the museum are amazing chaps. A life devoted to pure science seems to go hand in hand with great courtesy shown toward all humble seekers after knowledge. Nothing was too much trouble for them. First I was shown skulls dug up from ancient arctic Eskimo burial grounds.

As far as is known the Eskimos were the first people able to combat the cold without the use of firewood. At the end of three thousand years of Neolithic culture man had become sufficiently skillful in the production of tools so that he had reached the farthest northern border of land that could be cultivated. There he taught the forest people how to use his tools and make shelters, and sleds and elaborate traps for hunting, and how to domesticate the reindeer. So hunters spread eastward from both sides of the Bering Sea, along the coast of Alaska into Canada and to Labrador and Greenland. Tools enabled them to survive the rigors of the climate. Soapstone could be carved into lamps and kettles. Pottery could be baked for the same purpose. In a treeless land they could now boil their food, using only blubber as fuel. Cooking food made it easier to get at the bone marrow, which furnished such splendid strength for the hunt. Food consisted of the fattest meat they could kill, along with a few berries and roots gathered during the short summer.

Under these conditions, judging from the condition of the ancient skulls, many of them died with sound teeth that had never ached.

But lest I become unduly enthusiastic on the subject of fat meat, I was also shown the skulls of some ancient pueblo-dwelling Indians dug up in the Southwest. The ashes of their campfires showed that they had access to some game animals, but in the main they lived on coarsely ground corn. The teeth in some skulls were just as sound as those found in the Eskimo skulls.

So apparently it was just a matter of the primitive nature of the food.

I left the museum determined to try primitive food as the essential part of any reducing routine that might be devised. Only, how much of such food was necessary to maintain strength and still permit weight loss?

No one knew then, and as far as I know, no one knows with certainty now. Some patients can lose weight while eating two pounds of meat at each meal, three times a day. It all depends upon the individual. Some can eat much more than others, and not gain. We heard of a woman down in Tierra del Fuego who, if she could get it, could demolish a whole twelve-pound goose at one sitting. Eskimos gorge themselves on walrus meat after a successful hunt, and yet the Eskimo is rarely obese. He has the biological trait of a fat-looking face, and this, with his bulky clothes, gives a mistaken impression of his body weight. Our old-time trappers in the West devoured enormous quantities of buffalo hump and tongue and still kept lean. There may be an upper level of meat intake where no one can lose, but I've never found it.

However, we do know how small a portion of meat can be eaten while regaining and maintaining health and at the same time losing weight. Much of the concern shown over nutrition has been with vitamin deficiency. In this country the real deficiency state is not due to lack of vitamins but to a lack of amino acids. We must get enough of these essential amino acids to keep our body cells in a state of good repair.

In the effort to work out an effective anti-obesity routine, and in an entirely arbitrary way, a half pound of fresh fat meat without salt was chosen to be eaten with each meal. Apparently it was a fortunate choice, for that is the amount I still recommend.

From what I have observed, a half pound of meat per meal is the minimum quantity needed to maintain the work of repair of body cells.

Trial-and-error work seemed to show that the proportion of lean and fat had to be about three to one. Fat by itself is not easily digested. It must be mixed with something else. So the portion of meat after cooking should consist of two ounces of attached fat and six ounces of lean.

Most fat people don't eat enough fat meat three times a day to start the fire that will burn off their own excess fat.

Chosen to accompany the meat at this time was a second item, which could be a choice between a hotel portion of ripe raw fruit, or a potato baked or boiled without salt. This took the place of bread. For the human animal potatoes seem a much more agreeable form of starch than wheat flour. A potato is not really a root. It is a buried stem. It seemed desirable to try the potato because of the ease with which it is digested.

I hoped the slight difference in starch content might be unimportant, and this proved to be true.

The third item allowed was a full cup of black coffee or clear tea, to add to the pleasure of eating.

That, along with a thirty-minute walk before breakfast, was the original routine. Over the years it has been modified. The coffee is now limited to one half cup with each meal, and not a drop between.

The reason for not allowing a coffee break seems to be this: there is a minute bit of carbohydrate (starch that turns to sugar) in coffee. Everything that is eaten or drunk goes right into the blood stream and the pancreas responds by producing a hormone called insulin. Insulin is an antagonist of pituitary juice. Pituitary juice activates the burning of stored fat, but to some extent it can be smothered by insulin.

No one knows exactly how much the demitasse of coffee allowed with a meal slows up weight loss, but certainly it helps secure co-operation from the patient and seems to make the meal of fat meat easier to swallow.

The last item selected for the routine was water.

Water is the most important food of all.

Why it seems necessary in weight reduction to complete the drinking of six glasses of water (taken between meals) by five o'clock in the afternoon is indeed a mystery. It is said that Rommel trained his desert Afrika Korps to be thirsty only at certain times. It does seem possible, after six weeks of the regime, to get people trying to lose weight over a sense of thirst late in the day. Most chemical reactions in the body take place only in the presence of water, and avoiding it completely after five o'clock in the evening apparently helps the anti-fat forces in the body to do their work.

Under research conditions the routine works. In the hospital, nurses see to it that the patients adhere to the prescribed regimen. The patients may be virtually imprisoned with all factors leading to reduction carefully controlled. Under certain circumstances visiting relatives are compelled to talk to patients through glass, in order to stop their devilish tendency to smuggle in salted peanuts.

It's a strange fact that even if a patient's life is imperiled by overweight their loving kin will continue to stuff them with lethal tidbits, if they can get away with it.

The first year of effort spent in applying this routine to obese patients in the office and clinic yielded bewildering results. Many of the patients easily lost an average of seven pounds a month. They might brag at the end of three days' time of a feeling of intense well-being.

This was still back in 1920, mind you. At that time we had little knowledge of the importance of amino acids in food. Only essential amino acids can build cells and make the repairs of breaking-down cells in the body. And fresh meat is the most readily available source of amino acids.

But that explanation was unknown at the time, and I listened with incredulity to tales of a feeling of well-being. In the past anyone who lost weight usually felt weak and hungry.

Some of the patients lost little or no weight, and a few even gained. The attempt to discover why this was so has occupied a large part of my interest and time for the last forty-two years, and has led to a settled conviction. These people could not sustain the physical and mental effort involved in following exact orders. How to circumvent them became a sort of passion with me, and gradually led to improved technique. The failure to follow exact orders was understandable of course. It was quite like my experience in commanding the gas hospital in wartime.

The inherent trouble in this particular treatment of obesity is the failure to follow all of the orders. This may result in insufficient weight loss or no weight loss at all.

For some years the number of patients who failed to lose weight properly continued to worry me. Then I had the good fortune to make a firm friend of a Canadian engineer, Mr. A. J. T. Taylor, who was an intimate friend and backer of Vilhjalmur Stefansson, the explorer and anthropologist.

Stefansson had finished up an interesting experiment on nutrition at Bellevue Hospital. The work had been supervised by the great biochemist, Eugene F. Du Bois, and a report[1] had been published. Stefansson had expended years in studying the culture of the arctic Eskimos. He ended up by copying their way of life, and at one time he and two companions spent many months on the sea ice, living only on the meat they could kill. A report of his adventures and observations was published in 1921, in a book called *The Friendly Arctic*.

When anyone interested in food asks me where he can read up on the subject, I tell them to start with that. Among other things Stefansson is a marvelous hunter endowed with a sort of homing instinct or sense of direction that enabled him to find his way back to camp through storms on the sea ice. The report on the food that sustained him in his explorations was received with skepticism. It was thought that he must have had access to caches of groceries left by previous arctic explorers, so a committee of eminent scientists invited Stefansson and one of his companions, Karsten Andersen, to spend a year under close observation at Bellevue, to check on the possibility of living well on nothing but meat. The kind of meat, which included marrow and brains and kidneys and fresh fish, was to be as the patients' appetites dictated.

[1] Walter S. McClellan and Eugene F. Du Bois, "Prolonged meat diets with a study of kidney function and ketosis," *Journal of Biological Chemistry*, July 1930.

On February 13, 1928, the experiment was started, and it concluded on March 29, 1929. The first three weeks were devoted to a study of their reactions to ordinary mixed food, such as most of us eat. Calorimetry studies, blood assays, and kidney function tests were made for controls.

Then Andersen was put on just the meat he liked and Stefansson, to his alarm, was put on only the leanest meat possible to obtain. This was because Du Bois had been told of a previous experience Stefansson had had in the Arctic. The fall migration of caribou had been missed. The animals on their return in the spring had exhausted their supply of fat. In spite of the caches groaning with lean meat starvation stalked the camp. Weakness, protuberant abdomens, and diarrhea developed. Access to fat saved their lives. This report had likewise been greeted with skepticism, so Stefansson was asked to start off the experiment with lean meat alone.

Within two days he had diarrhea and a feeling of baffling discomfort. Allowing him to eat fat again cleared up the symptoms in three days, and the experiment went on. The daily intake of food they chose to eat was estimated as follows: the protein content varied from 100 to 140 grams. The fat from 200 to 300 grams. The carbohydrate, derived entirely from the meat, from 7 to 12 grams. This represented an average intake of 2000 to 3100 calories. At the end of a year the subjects were mentally alert, physically active, and showed no evidence of damaged organs. Perhaps the most remarkable thing about the whole experiment was the co-operation afforded the scientists by two men of such high caliber.

Throughout the test, the total acidity of the urine was two or three times over that on mixed diets. Acetone was constantly present, apparently without any ill effects.

I had observed two families, in practice, that bothered me. Several members of each family were fat and had come to me for treatment. Fast weight reduction was in order, so they were given only two things with a meal, fat meat and black coffee. Both families seemed to have an inherent inability to convert protein into some carbohydrate, if that was the difficulty. They developed acidosis to the extent of a very offensive dead-violet odor on the breath and some sense of weakness. Switching over to slow weight reduction with three things with a meal had instantly resolved the difficulty. But why had it existed?

Oh, there were dozens of questions I wanted to discuss with Stefansson, so Fred Taylor brought him out to my home on Long Island. Some steamed clams and a good steak loosened him up, and we sat around a beach fire and talked for hours. He proved to be a mine of information. As I remember his conversation, it went something like this:

"Well, in the first place, it is just as well to have intelligent companions if you expect to live for long periods on sea ice. It isn't enough to pick up, at Point Barrow, a dock hand who is somewhat inured to cold weather. Men you take with you have no worry about scurvy. They know that fresh meat and fish entirely prevent that. And they know that there is always fresh water on the sea ice. They may be doubtful at first over their ability to get along without a few luxuries. At the end of several weeks the extras are discarded as not worth the effort of transporting.

"Most people enjoy fresh fat meat from the start, but some react this way: they are expected to live on thin slivers of fat seal meat and the broth it is cooked in, and this is eagerly taken at first and then with increasing reluctance on the second and third day. By the fourth day the pieces of meat may be found on the snow or given to the dogs. For two or three days these men seem to eat almost nothing. Then appetite for the meat comes with a rush and no more trouble is ex-

perienced. After many months away from a base where there
are grocery stores, elaborate menus may be planned against
the day of return. During their time away they have been
free from head colds, but as soon as they return to people
who have been living on groceries, head colds are promptly
contracted. A few days of living on the food they thought
would be so wonderful usually finds them back in the Eskimo
part of town trying to beg, borrow, or steal some delicious
fat from the back of the eyes of a caribou, or else some good
seal meat. Accustomed to fat in their food, their bodies seem
to crave it, and groceries do not satisfy.

"It is highly desirable to be a good rifle shot so that a seal
may be shot through the head. Matches must be most carefully conserved. The technique of meal preparation is exact.
Hollow bones and strips of blubber cut like bacon are saved
from the day before. A pyramid is formed of the hollow
bones. At the apex the strips of blubber are laid. A little piece
of shirttail or similar cloth is reserved to help start each meal.
The cloth is impregnated with fat and laid under the pyramid
of bones. The cloth should light with one match. Exposed to
this heat, the blubber melts and runs down over the bones,
which act as a wick. This fat burns with an intensely hot but
smoky flame. Over this a preferably unwelded solid metal container is placed, filled with water and thin slivers of fat meat.
By the time the water boils, the meat is cooked and ready to
eat. The broth it is cooked in is drunk and is much more
satisfying than tea or coffee."

So that was the way of it, was it? Just be sure you are right
and then be tough about it. What was I worrying about? If
Stefansson could get his people to live that way, I certainly
should have enough executive ability to get my patients to
stick to a beautifully broiled sirloin and a demitasse of black
coffee.

In the long run hospital treatment for overweight patients is unsatisfactory. The nurse wakens the patient after eight hours; they walk thirty minutes at a measured rate, the food is weighed and no salt is allowed, the water is exact, weight loss is exact, et cetera. And it doesn't mean a thing. As soon as the patient leaves the hospital, all of the weight that has been lost is promptly regained. The patient hasn't learned to withstand temptation by unaided effort.

In treating the obese, it is necessary for the doctor to be on guard against the liars. There are some patients who will look you in the eye and swear that as God is their witness they have eaten only what you have ordered. The scale has another story to tell. It is understandable, but a waste of everybody's time.

If worst comes to worst, and the patient can afford it, three shifts of nurses, each on eight-hour duty, are sent to the house. The nurses are instructed to watch everything but to criticize nothing. At the end of the week they report. And the average number of errors made by one patient who was gaining two pounds a week on a reducing routine was seventy-seven.

Astonishing things show up, like the disappearance of a whole box of crackers every day. A half pound of soda mints may be devoured. The level of a bottle of Dubonnet steadily lowers. A salty toothpaste is used or coffee is sipped between meals. The patient won't set an alarm clock, or carry a watch on the walk, and so it goes.

There is a limit to patience of course. The physician may have made an error in sizing up the patient in the first place. Some people can't sustain any kind of effort and it is wrong to badger them.

Routinely, I have failed to get good results with professional artists in the music world. I've become quite embittered about it.

There is a reason for it. Talent at the professional level means an overdevelopment of one part of the brain. Nature seems to compensate for that by taking away some other quality. So that economic sense or the ability to sustain effort is lacking. It is not too important. Such people give us a great deal of pleasure and get a lot of joy out of life for themselves as long as they last.

All the more credit is due to that splendid seventy-five per cent majority of patients who do not falter.

The younger the patient, the better. Each year that passes after the age of thirty-three makes it more difficult to lose weight, and adequate outdoor exercise, strict prohibition of salt, a measured time in bed, and a measured intake of water become increasingly important. At any age, it seems possible to lose weight, once you make up your mind.

The cells of the body have to grow rapidly up to the age of thirty-three. After that, when hardening of the arteries sets in, as it does with all of us, the cells must be repaired. There is little in the food we take in that has the ability to grow cells and repair cells except essential amino acids. These are most readily available in fresh fat meat.

Everything goes back or rather forward to enough amino acids in food.

Some observers may think that feeding fat people a lower limit of one half pound of fresh fat meat with each meal, and allowing them to take as much more as is wanted, is after all another form of low-calorie diet. That criticism misses the point and seems to me to be based on the old idea that calories are interchangeable, whether derived from protein, or fat, or carbohydrate. For fresh meat contains all of the ten essential amino acids without which cell growth and cell repair cannot take place.

Keep this premise always in mind: enough fresh meat is

needed so that the ten essential amino acids contained in it can grow and repair cells, and there must be on the meat enough of the fat that is necessary for muscular work and to insure one bowel movement a day.

This was the "strong medicine" prepared to fight obesity and its associated members of the "obesity sextette."

Chapter V

THE CAUSES OF
OBESITY

CONTINUOUS SUCCESS in any line of endeavor, including weight reduction, demands rigid adherence to biological laws. Biology is the big thing, and medicine ranks only as a small subdivision of biology.

During the millions of years that our ancestors lived by hunting, every weakling who could not maintain perfect health on fresh fat meat and water was bred out.

There are probably only two perfect foods—fresh fat meat and clean water.

Whenever you are in a jam with the human body, it is well to go back to the common inheritance of mankind. People have only been eating junk for eight thousand years, and that is a fleabite in evolution. An evolutionary process takes a million years.

Any food used in the treatment of obesity should be normal to begin with, and only fresh fat meat and water come within the strict limits. However, anything else that can be eaten and still permit a weight loss of three pounds a week is legitimate. I haven't found much else that will fit into the category except a demitasse of coffee with each meal.

The main weapons in the prevention and treatment of disease and human carelessness will probably always be food and exercise.

To my thinking the greatest advance in recorded medical history is the thirty-minute walk before breakfast. Premiums for life insurance are usually paid for the benefit of someone else. If you want any life insurance for yourself you had better pay the daily premium of a thirty-minute walk.

As I said before, it is strong medicine, and not for the weak of will.

People are all different, which tends to make life interesting. Some succeed in weight reduction just as easily as others fail. Combating those with a tendency to fail takes twice the work. Let's take a couple of illustrations.

A typically successful patient is a man named Stebbins who climbed on my office scales the other day and watched the resultant numerals with an expression of complete amazement. At the age of fifty Mr. Stebbins had been fighting a steadily increasing waistline for seventeen years.

The scale registered one hundred and sixty-four and a half pounds as against one hundred and sixty-five pounds four weeks before.

"I didn't believe it was possible," the patient muttered. "This weight reduction business has finally reached the stage of a mathematical certainty if you do exactly as you're told."

Mr. Stebbins had just proven that his weight was at last within normal limits by eating four things with a meal, having one two-ounce drink before dinner, and showing no gain in weight at the end of four weeks.

Twenty-one weeks before he had puffed into the office with a body weight of two hundred and ten pounds, and radiating skepticism from every pore. I had told him that some executive ability was a great help in weight reduction, and because he was the chief chemist in a large organization he must have some of that quality. For fifteen weeks he would be required to eat enough of a big fat steak broiled with pepper, but no salt, and a demitasse of black coffee, to show a gain of at least one half pound on an accurate scale directly after completion of the meal. That probably meant that a porterhouse steak should weigh about one and a half pounds to begin with. This meal was to be eaten three times a day.

Sleep was to be regulated by an alarm clock for eight hours or less, but there must be no hurry in the morning. Deep restful sleep for eight, or seven, or six hours is difficult for some people to achieve because they insist upon waking up naturally. Then the last four hours are too close to the conscious level to be particularly restful. The regular setting of an alarm clock and lying there till it goes off results in something called autohypnosis and, with training, can result in much deeper sleep.

Mr. Stebbins had to allow thirty minutes to shave and dress, thirty minutes to walk outdoors on level ground, and thirty minutes to eat breakfast and read the newspaper. Between meals it was necessary to drink six tumblers of water, three between breakfast and lunch and three between lunch and dinner. He was not to drink water after five o'clock in the afternoon. If he was thirsty after dinner he could rinse his mouth out but should not swallow any water. If he was not going to be at home for lunch, he should broil his own steak in his laboratory. Restaurant chefs are too likely to lie about salt. Nothing was allowed between meals except water and any cold fresh meat roasted without salt that he might want. At an evening party there was nothing he could hold in his hand, not even water. His bread eating was over for all time. When his weight was normal he might be able to burn up one two-ounce drink of liquor and still keep normal. Until then no liquor of any kind was allowed. Every two weeks for fifteen weeks he would have to come into the office to see that he had lost six pounds. Nothing was to be done about constipation for the first four days.

Even with his intensely orderly mind he missed the goal of normal weight in fifteen weeks by six weeks. On three of his visits to the office he showed no weight loss and felt discouraged. But fortunately each time the error was easily discovered. The first time he hadn't bothered to eat breakfast, hoping to lose faster. Instead the fire went out, his stored fat did not burn, and he didn't lose anything.

The second time it was discovered that he was having a coffee break in the laboratory, and the minute bit of carbohydrate in the coffee between meals had put the fire out.

He was heartily ashamed of the third error, which turned out to be a bottle of ginger ale every afternoon, taken because the weather was hot.

But Mr. Stebbins hadn't done a bad job at all considering everything, and he had learned a lot. It takes real intestinal fortitude to lose weight properly.

"Doctor," he asked, "have you time to talk a little? I'd like to ask you some questions." A new patient had just called up to cancel an appointment so I told him to go ahead.

"When I first came in, I didn't tell you that life insurance statistics on obesity had thrown a scare into me and that I'd been to four other doctors before I came to you. I want to know why they couldn't get a pound in weight off of me. What was wrong?" he asked.

"What did they tell you to do?" I inquired.

"Well, the first one practically told me to forget it, because some people are fat and some are thin and nature violently resists any effort to change the situation. That explanation was no help to me so I quit him right away."

"Yes," I told him. "That was the old medical idea that stopped progress in the treatment of obesity for many years. Nature does resist change, unless food is normal to begin with. When we go back to first principles in eating, it has been determined, the tendency to remain in balance can be easily upset and without hunger."

"The second man put me on a low-calorie diet," he went on, "and told me it was just a matter of arithmetic. If I ate less than I burned up I had to lose. As a matter of fact I gained six pounds while he was treating me. Why was that?"

"What else did you eat beside the low-calorie diet?" I asked him.

"Twice a day, because I felt too weak to even think, I made some whole wheat toast in the laboratory," was his response.

"That's just the point," I told him. "People practically always steal food when they are hungry, and low-calorie diets mean weakness and hunger. I have observed one man who successfully lost weight on a low-calorie diet, but he was an engineer with a will of iron. And even he regained most of the weight lost within a year's time. No! Counting calories is for the birds. There should be no sensation of hunger in proper weight reduction. You weren't hungry at any time during the last twenty-one weeks, were you?"

"No," he admitted, "just the normal good appetite for meals, and I never had recourse to the cold fat meat you allowed me between meals."

"What about the third doctor?" I asked.

"He took a metabolism test in his office and told me I was minus thirty-two, and that the secretion from the thyroid gland in my neck was insufficient to burn my body fat properly. He started me in on a grain of thyroid extract three times a day and gradually ran it up to four grains three times a day, but I kept on gaining weight. I felt too jumpy to continue with him.

"Dr. Donaldson, you didn't even take a metabolism test and told me in the X-ray room that my thyroid was normal. How did you arrive at that conclusion?"

A sensible question it was. A lot of patients are smart when you come right down to it. I told Mr. Stebbins:

"In the first place you didn't notice that before I made that remark in the X-ray room after fluoroscopic examination of your heart, I had already done three other things. I talked to you and noted that you were mentally alert. I looked for the amount and texture of your hair, and I had you remove your shoes and socks and felt of your feet. When there is a real lack of the thyroid extract it is shown by a rather stupid mentality, sparse hair of a certain texture, cold feet, and a heart that has the shape of a deer hunter's woolen sock. You had none of those findings. At times thyroid extract can increase the cooking flame in the body, just as new sparkplugs may increase the efficiency of an automobile engine. It used to be thought that feeding it in small quantities might help to burn off excess body weight. With the exception of about four per cent, that happened regularly to people with the disease called exophthalmic goiter. They would usually melt away under the load of too much thyroid hormone in the blood. But it didn't work in simple obesity. Because so many thousands of fat people still uselessly take thyroid extract to lose weight, the subject needs to be more generally understood."

I went on to explain that as insufficient function of the thyroid began to be recognized and studied perhaps undue attention was paid to it. Numerically it has never been important, and for some unknown reason seems to occur with steadily less frequency. Children can be born with a condition called cretinism. Frequently they are dwarfs and fail to develop sexually and mentally. Treatment with thyroid extract is not particularly rewarding. They may become only a little less stupid.

A lack of thyroid secretion in adults is called myxedema. Usually it appears without obvious cause, but it can develop after removal of too much of the thyroid gland in an operation for exophthalmic goiter. In myxedema the metabolism and mental reactions are slowed. The victims may gain weight from retained water and have skin that becomes rough and dry and hair that becomes sparse.

Everyone who is growing bald hopes that something wrong can be demonstrated with the thyroid gland, and that the administration of thyroid extract may result in luxuriant hair growth. It is a slim hope indeed. Baldness is inevitable if one has that kind of grandparents.

Decreased sexual desire, irregular periods, and sterility can also occur in myxedema. Such things are of common occurrence in medicine so that the field is wide open for the abuse of thyroid extract. Unfortunately it only works in that rare condition, true myxedema. A good physical examination is usually sufficient to rule that out.

Reports of a "low metabolism" obtained in a medical office should be treated with skepticism. The possibilities for technical error are too great when small portable machines are used, and scientific work based on such reports has little value. Cameron V. Bailey, the physicist, has quit practice now, and more is the pity. Perhaps no other individual has done more to straighten out medical thinking on metabolism reports than Bailey. For many years he conducted the meta-

bolic work at the New York Post Graduate Medical School
and Hospital.

Using the Tissot method and with specially designed apparatus, he was able to measure heat production in the body
with a high degree of accuracy. He taught us that a laboratory
test is as much a test of the laboratory as it is of the patient.
The apparatus used was of necessity cumbersome, and the
patients tested had to be at complete mental and physical rest.
In securing these conditions Bailey was a past master. When
there is a deficient supply of thyroid in the body, as in true
myxedema, a daily dose of a grain to a grain and a half will
correct all the symptoms that can be corrected. More than
that may have a poisonous effect.

The body seems to have a great safety factor in normal
people and in cases of simple obesity with no demonstrable
metabolic defect. If no extra thyroid extract is needed a person's own thyroid gland slows down and makes less, or else
the body destroys the excess amount. In normal people monstrous quantities, at times up to five grains of thyroid extract
three times a day, can be taken with no apparent ill effect
and particularly no weight loss. So that if a fat man or woman
is taking more than a grain and a half in any twenty-four-hour
period he or she probably doesn't need it at all. Because extra
thyroid hormone is not needed, the body destroys it.

"Now, what about the last doctor you went to?" I asked
Mr. Stebbins.

His answer was, "That was a miserable experience. His
only interest seemed to be in cholesterol. I had innumerable
examinations to determine the cholesterol level, while I lived
mostly on rice and corn oil and kept on gaining weight. What
is all this propaganda about cholesterol anyway? The reaction
I had was that I never want to see rice or corn oil again as
long as I live."

I explained: "A sterol called cholesterol is supposed to be guilty of making us grow old before our time. But there is no proof of this. Cholesterol is formed from breakdown products of fat, or protein, or carbohydrate—all of them. These three major food substances break down to active acetate, and cholesterol is built up from this.

"The cholesterol blood level is raised by coconut oil, milk fat, and egg yolk. It is lowered by corn oil, cottonseed oil, safflower oil, and unhydrogenated peanut oil. Olive oil and meat fats have little effect on the cholesterol level.

"Even if meat fat did increase cholesterol, people don't stop to realize that cholesterol is an important constituent of the framework of all living cells. It is from this framework that many life processes proceed. Cholesterol is closely related to the vitamin D which prevents rickets and enters into the formation of bile acids and sex hormones.

"No, we would be in bad shape indeed if it wasn't for cholesterol. Because some of it is found in the broken-down material in rotten arteries, and some families with a tendency to coronary artery disease show increased blood levels of it, cholesterol has been made a whipping boy, which is unjustified.

"Since the determination of its importance much of the research work on cholesterol has been abandoned, though some is still going on. Talk about cholesterol is old hat, forget it, and certainly it would never help you with weight reduction."

"That clears up those points," the patient said. "Now would you mind telling me how I differ chemically from ordinary people who eat and drink much more than I do and never seem to gain a pound?"

"If you are that much interested," I told him, "you had better go up to the library of the Academy and do a little reading. First get hold of Godlowski's article.[1] That is hard reading, but there is some stuff by Pennington which you will find fascinating." It is only in the last two decades that research men have begun to come up with the answer to the question of why some clinicians feed fat to reduce weight. Perhaps the greatest credit for co-ordinating the reports of the scientists, and for producing a sensible explanation of the mechanism of obesity, belongs to Dr. A. W. Pennington of the medical division of E. I. du Pont de Nemours and Company in Wilmington, Delaware. He is dead now, which is a sadness. In a symposium on obesity[2] he gives an excellent outline of his ideas on the subject.

Experts on nutrition who had gone before were handicapped in two notable ways. The first was their inability to think in a biological manner.

Hindsight is easy, of course, but it does seem queer that in the old days no one ever stopped to think that man has been a hunter since his beginning. Food was the primary concern of man as he evolved, and it had to be right. He lived on the fattest meat he could kill and on water. The women gathered roots and berries when times were hard.

In those million years every weakling who could not maintain perfect health on that food was bred out. Man didn't fool around in the old days. If he couldn't leap six feet straight up in the air to catch the branch of a tree, some saber-toothed tiger was likely to solve all of his problems. The ability to live well on meat and water is the common inheritance of mankind. It is only in the last eight thousand years since man turned to agriculture for a stable food supply that we have had trouble with eating.

[1] Z. Godlowski, "Carbohydrate metabolism in obesity," *Edinburgh Medical Journal*, 53 (1946), 574.
[2] A. W. Pennington, *New England Journal of Medicine*, 248 (June 4, 1953), 959–64.

But until recently this idea was too simple and too big for observers to encompass. And for many years it was thought that life is insupportable on anything but a mixed and mainly carbohydrate diet. The second great difficulty the experts were confronted with was the lack of one proper tool. What happens to food after it is taken into the body and before it is excreted was a good deal of a mystery. The discovery that tracer elements, called radioactive isotopes, could be added to food and then followed through the body opened the door to the knowledge of how food is burned or stored. Stored fat in the body used to be considered a lifeless mass but now, thanks to the isotopes, we know that it is constantly being built up and broken down with resultant complete change every three weeks. Fatty tissue is alive.

Pennington's great contribution was to run through the chain of command in the chemical changes of carbohydrate and fat once they enter the body. Some of the carbohydrate may not be absorbed from the intestine. Then it goes on to fermentation by intestinal bacteria. There is no juice in the body of anything living that will split cellulose. The food value in cellulose has to be liberated under the rotting effect of bacteria. Whole populations of non-humans, older and more efficient than our civilization, have been built up on the splitting of cellulose for food. Maeterlinck described it in *The Life of the White Ant*. As a result of the fermentation in the bowel, acetic acid, lactic acid, butyric acid, succinic acid, carbon dioxide, alcohol, and hydrogen can all be liberated. This would seem to explain one thing that obese patients on a high-fat-and-protein, low-carbohydrate intake all remark on three days after the start of the new routine. Intestinal gases which may have plagued them for years seem to disappear, for the eliminated carbohydrate foods have cellulose as a framework.

Once absorbed, the various starches and sugars are changed to glucose, a simple type of sugar that circulates in the blood. Thus, after a person eats carbohydrate, his blood is found to contain a higher concentration of sugar than before. The excess sugar is soon withdrawn from the blood. The liver converts some of it to glycogen, or "animal starch," which is stored in liver and muscles, and an even greater quantity is quickly converted to fat. The liver changes sugar into fat, and, probably even more important than this, a person's own fatty deposits engage actively in converting to fat the sugar that is brought to them in the blood. In this way the amount of sugar in the blood is kept at a constant level.

In the muscles, glycogen serves as a storehouse of energy that can be released as required. The energy is released by means of a series of chemical reactions that are made possible by enzymes, the catalytic agents that operate in the cells of all living things. More than a dozen chemical steps can be counted when glycogen is being broken down to yield its energy but there are three main stages in the process. First, glycogen must be broken down to form pyruvic acid; second, the pyruvic acid must be broken down to something called active acetate; and third, the active acetate is combusted to carbon dioxide and water.

As long as the enzymes are working properly all goes well. When one enzyme is missing or is insufficient in quantity, however, the result can be compared to a bottleneck or log jam. If, for example, an enzyme necessary for the conversion of pyruvic acid to active acetate is lacking, pyruvic acid accumulates. It is possible that the inherited factor in obesity is the lack of such an enzyme.

Pyruvic acid is a substance of crucial importance biologically. Here it stands on the main highway of the chemical breakdown of glycogen for energy. But it stands at an inter-

section on the highway; there is another road that it can follow—the road to fat formation. If pyruvic acid becomes
blocked in its progress toward complete combustion it becomes converted into fat. The fat, of course, can then be
burned for energy, in the form of fatty acids and ketones;
but the accumulated pyruvic acid has a chemical effect that
dampens the flame. As a result, fat tends to build up in the
body. In brief, sugar and starchy meals produce obesity in a
person who suffers from a lack of the enzyme needed for the
chemical breakdown of pyruvic acid.

In such a person, sugar and starchy meals have additional
effects that aid and abet the weight-gaining process. Sugar
and starch stimulate the pancreas to form large amounts of
insulin, and insulin speeds up the conversion of sugar into fat.
Also, insulin opposes the action of the master gland, the
pituitary, whose active fat-mobilizing principle ordinarily in-
sures the smooth breakdown of fat for energy.

Medical men, interested in weight reduction, take a dim
view of that one piece of whole wheat toast that fat people
love to steal while on a reducing regime. It isn't the caloric
value of the wrong thing that bothers. One piece of toast
can raise the levels of pyruvic acid and insulin in the blood
and stop excess fat from burning.

When plenty of fat is eaten with a meal, however, the
pituitary hormone that promotes the breakdown of stored fat
is stimulated.

Fat enters the blood stream as fatty acids, simple and combined. The liver breaks these down into ketones which re-
enter the blood and circulate to the tissues. Fatty acids and
ketones when burned in the body furnish, just as glycogen
does, the energy for heat and for muscular work. But there
may be only about fourteen ounces of stored glycogen for
reserve energy. That amount can easily be exhausted. Reserve

fat, which can be converted into valuable fatty acids and ketones, may amount to a great many pounds. In the old days
of periodic famine a certain amount of obesity was probably
a desirable trait. Excess fat was a first-rate storage reservoir
for energy. Glycogen furnishes perhaps the best energy for
quick action, but it is fatty acids and ketones from fat that
we have to depend upon for the long pull. As they burn, excess body fat disappears.

Ketones, while they are valuable sources of energy, are also
fairly strong organic acids capable of slightly disturbing the
acid base regulation in the body. The importance of feeding
protein along with fat seems to lie in its wonderful ability
to repair the cells in the liver and protect them from damage.

The liver is probably the most important organ we have.
The faulty idea that it is necessary to eat plenty of carbohydrate along with fat in order to prevent acidosis has little
place in the proper treatment of obesity.

It seems to me that there are three horns to the dilemma
of the fat man.

He can go ahead and enjoy himself on the mainly carbohydrate food he has been trained to like. If he eats all
he wants he will probably have strength enough to work. The
reason to live is to be happy, and many of us get a lot of
happiness out of freedom from a sense of government. The
only trouble is that the fat man is inconsistent. When the
high mortality rate in obesity catches up with him, which it
inevitably does, and he starts to die, he wants something done
about it, but fast. And it may be too late.

Or he can do what most fat people do, which is to halfway
follow a low-calorie diet which is mainly carbohydrate. This
will result in hunger and weakness and at the end of the year
he will weigh just the same or more. Because low-calorie

diets are the custom the neighbors will approve of this procedure and give him lots of sympathy. And who doesn't like
sympathy? Also the neighbors will do their level best to get
him to break his so-called diet with tempting special birth-
day cakes and strawberry shortcakes. Then they will laugh at
him afterward. This is in the nature of things.

Or he can get tough and stick to a big fat steak and a half
cup of black coffee three times a day. That will pull on his
stored fat and burn it as fatty acids and ketones, with plenty
of energy and a sense of well-being, freedom from hunger,
and a loss in weight of three pounds a week.

In doing this he will be somewhat in the class of a pioneer,
and a pioneer always meets with suspicion. No matter how
well he does, he need not expect the approval of his neighbors.
Any disaster that may overtake him, even to the extent of
ground moles getting in his lawn, will be blamed on his "red
meat" diet. Physicians don't care whether the meat is red,
white, or blue as long as it has fat on it, and is healthy, and
tastes good, and there is plenty of it.

The fat man has to make up his mind whether to crack
up on glycogen from carbohydrate or to live well on ketones
and fatty acids from fat meat.

Obesity is just as simple and just as complicated as that.

The same basic principles apply to the treatment of all
types of obesity, but details can vary depending on the mentality of the individual. Let's see what happens to a much
less intelligent and much more emotional overweight patient.
It seems indicated to lay down the law in just as arbitrary a
fashion as did Moses.

Mrs. Blankenship was a fat young woman with two children. Several times during the course of questioning she dis-
solved into tears—which isn't good. Emotional instability always adds to difficulties. Apparently she had plenty of reason

to think that her husband was running around with a series of secretaries, and she was meditating divorce. Physical examination showed nothing more than overweight and the big pupils and fast heart rate that go with an unstable nervous system.

So, bearing in mind that patients seem to comprehend only five per cent of any spoken advice, you ring for the secretary and dictate a letter. The patient had failed to lose weight while under the care of other physicians. A different and rather shocking approach was needed.

"Dear Mrs. Blankenship:

"You have a diagnosis of:

(1) Simple obesity

(2) Nervousness

"Your weight of one hundred and ninety pounds is considered to be fifty-four pounds too much. The fastest rate you can expect to lose weight is three pounds a week, for you want your skin to follow the fat so you won't be wrinkled when you get through. That means eighteen weeks of grueling effort on your part. Most women, and you are among them, only have two problems. Should they weigh one hundred and thirty-six pounds dressed, or one hundred and thirty pounds dressed? You are in the one-hundred-and-thirty-six-pound class and I expect you to be there on the fourth day of September. As to your marital relations, remember this: you are not going to get anywhere in this life if you avoid facing up to facts.

"You were the one that married a man with a roving eye. A polygamous tendency is probably an inherited trait from a grandparent. If you lose your looks after you get married, you can expect just one result.

"Some of your concern over the future of the children is unjustified. Whether or not they turn out to be the love-them-and-leave-them type has already been decided by the grandparents. A good deal of this talk about broken homes is rubbish as far as the children are concerned. Environment is little more than five per cent of the factors that determine destiny.

"Your husband, in many respects, seems to be a good man. I advise you to compete fiercely for his attentions, by regaining your looks. Nothing else is going to work. Bear in mind what happened in the Roman Senate many centuries ago. For two years the senators are supposed to have debated the question as to whether or not women had any brains at all. Cicero is credited with winding up the argument by saying, 'Well, gentlemen, what of it?' My advice to you is to keep away from lawyers and go to work.

"You are going to have to burn your own fat off in the flame of fat meat. You have five potent enemies, equal in strength. They are:

(1) The failure to walk thirty minutes without stopping, before breakfast, unless it is raining or snowing at that time.

(2) Flour

(3) Salt

(4) Sugar

(5) Alcohol

"Attack the problem this way. Get your own alarm clock, and set it to go off forty-five minutes before your husband arises. Allow yourself eight hours or less in bed. Take fifteen minutes to dress for the street. Wear a ski suit in winter and long johns if they are needed to keep warm. Mittens are better than gloves. Buy a police whistle from a hardware store and wear it around your neck in plain sight. Don't carry a handbag. You don't want to get beaten up. Then walk thirty minutes without stopping. You don't expect to lose weight the first ten minutes of the walk. It is the last twenty that do the business.

"Be home in time to spend fifteen minutes getting your husband's and the children's breakfast. Then get your own.

"For eighteen weeks, and three hundred and seventy-eight consecutive meals, eat nothing but two double rib Frenched lamb chops with pepper on them, and a demitasse of real black coffee without sugar. Have a measured quantity of water between meals. Three tumblers between breakfast and lunch and three between lunch and dinner, finishing by five o'clock.

"If you are going to be away from home at lunchtime, broil four chops at breakfast. Allow two to get cold after cooking and wrap them in Saran or aluminum foil. Don't eat in a restaurant for eighteen weeks. If you are still hungry after eating two chops, you can have as many more as are desired. But no extra coffee is allowed. There is a minute quantity of starch in coffee. And any starch, particularly between meals, makes it difficult to lose weight. Your ancestors, for about a million years and up to eight thousand years ago, lived almost exclusively on the fattest meat they could kill, and on water. That is your inheritance, and you can safely do the same thing.

"Your bowels may only move once or twice the first week, three times the second week, and every day on the third week. Do nothing about them, except to eat more fat on the meat if they are not moving every day.

"Expect to come in the office after the first three days on this food, and then every fourteen days from then on until weight is normal. The reason for that is because most people like you will begin to steal food on the fifteenth day unless checked by a physician.

"Try not to make stupid mistakes. It is too bad if cooking chops at breakfast nauseates you. Just hold your nose. If you lose a meal, go right back at it the next meal.

"Remember that grapefruit and all other raw fruit is starch. You can't have any.

"There is enough sugar in a piece of chewing gum to stop weight loss. Avoid seltzer and all carbonated drinks. Avoid Dubonnet and sherry and cider and grape juice as you would the Devil. They are all alcoholic, and weight loss is impossible when you take alcohol.

"Your flour and sugar days are over for the rest of your life. If you want one particular thing to blame your sorrows on it is that piece of whole wheat toast you have been eating for breakfast.

"No breadstuff means any kind of bread. The darker it is the worse it seems. Diabetic biscuits and crackers, whole wheat toast and Danish pastry, gluten bread, Ry Krisp, waffles, pancakes, the dressing in fowl, flour gravy, sandwiches, all cakes, and pie crust are in the same category. They must go out of your life, now and forever.

"Now let's see how much spunk you have!"

The arbitrary nature of that letter needs explanation. She was the emotional type. Her orders had to be exact, with no loopholes.

It was a pretty rough way to treat a nice girl. But it worked. The family is happy today. She even wangled her husband into taking her into a Fifth Avenue store and buying her a complete new wardrobe when she reached one hundred and thirty-six pounds. She maintained that weight easily when shifted to four items with each meal.

Women are smart when they avoid a frontal attack on a

husband. Almost any good man will feel his back hair stand up when a woman uses a frontal attack. Women are supposed to gain their ends by indirection, and by being charming if it kills them.

Chapter VI

HEART DISEASE

MOST OF US are born with a pump that is designed to contract efficiently anywhere from forty to one hundred and thirty times a minute for sixty-seven years. After that, any work one gets out of it is profit. Carrying around fifteen pounds of extra fat all day long is the equivalent in foot-pounds of energy of shoveling two tons of coal. Such useless wear and tear needs to be avoided.

Always, the best illustrations of medical teaching are to be found in the office files. Names and a few details have been changed to avoid any possible embarrassment to living patients.

A Mr. Thomas, an obese middle-aged man, walked into my waiting room supporting himself on the arm of his chauffeur. The walk into the examining room made him puff for breath. On the way to his office in the car, pain in the chest had forced him to take a nitroglycerine tablet. That had given him a bursting sensation in his head, and he decided to come in to see me.

The family history recorded a number of overweight brothers and sisters. They seemed to have run the whole gamut of the complications of obesity.

His personal history showed that he had gained weight steadily since leaving college. He had always been a big bread eater. At the age of fifty he weighed two hundred and ten pounds and had developed shortness of breath on the stairs. By the time he was fifty-five, shortness of breath would awaken him in the middle of the night. Then terrifying dreams developed. Usually they involved his chauffeur, who seemed to be chasing him with an ax. He had fired two chauffeurs but that didn't help. On two occasions swollen ankles had caused him to seek hospital admission. Each time he had received injections of a powerful mercurial. That got rid of a lot of urine and swelling but had left him feeling shattered. He was afraid to take any more. Many reducing diets had been tried but all had failed. His present trouble was the pain in the chest, which had developed in the last week. A full meal, or a slight grade, or walking against a wind could induce it.

Physical examination showed a rather short thick-necked individual with a ruddy face. His body weight was two hundred and sixteen pounds. The heart sounds were barely audible and of poor quality, but the fluoroscope showed only moderate enlargement. His liver was considerably enlarged but not tender. The ankles were swollen and albumen was present in his urine. The electrocardiogram showed only changes proportionate to his age. He had not as yet had coronary thrombosis.

So I summoned the secretary and, since this was serious, took plenty of time.

"Dear Mr. Thomas," I dictated.

"You have a diagnosis today of:

"(1) Obesity with a fatty liver, and (2) arteriosclerotic heart disease. If you ever want to straighten this heart out, you will have to reach the ringside weight that you would fight at in Madison Square Garden. That means one inch of loose fat on your lower abdomen and a dressed weight of one hundred and fifty-four pounds. An average weight loss of three pounds a week is as fast as you can be safely reduced. That means keeping your nose right on the grindstone for twenty-one weeks. You can blame your difficulties on flour and sugar and the failure to exercise. Unless you are willing to stop eating flour now and forever, I don't want to take care of you. If you continue your one piece of protein bread for breakfast, there is nothing ahead of you but disaster.

"Apparently a lot of fatty changes have gone on in your blood vessels and this has been followed by a moderate enlargement of your heart. I said moderate. If the enlargement was marked, there would not be much hope of helping you. But, with moderate enlargement, your heart may improve as your weight comes down. That heart was designed to pump around a man who weighs one hundred and fifty-four pounds. When the overload is markedly reduced, it may work better.

"The nightmares you have been having are due to back pressure from the failing heart. Carbon dioxide is not washed out of your brain at a proper rate. Sleep as high as you can. Even a rocking chair at night might be safer and more comfortable than the bed. The liver is swollen from fat rather than with back pressure from a failing heart. That kind of a liver is just like *pâté de foie gras*, and comes from years of gluttony. Bread addiction is little different from that of alcohol or cocaine or heroin addiction, and sometimes it seems even more dangerous. Did you ever see a fat man praying for the soul of some poor alcoholic or drug addict? Yet he couldn't stop his own helping of whole wheat toast for breakfast to save his soul.

"This heart of yours has been sufficiently damaged to make it unsafe to ever again climb a flight of stairs or hill. The trouble with an enlarged heart is this: each individual muscle fiber is supplied by its own little blood vessel. When the muscle fiber enlarges the blood supply should also be increased, but it isn't. So the muscle is relatively dry.

"Normally, what happens when you safely climb stairs is this: seventeen times as much blood flows through the wall of your heart, and your blood pressure goes up forty points. If you can only deliver fourteen times the amount of blood needed when at rest, the back of your knees feel weak. At thirteen times, you will be short of breath. At eleven times, you will have pain in the chest. At nine times, over you go as dead as a mackerel.

"It is that simple, and that dangerous. Most organs in the body are built seventeen times stronger than they need to be. So that you can damage a heart a lot and then, if you have the good sense to live within your limits, you can still carry on.

"Your routine is to be as simple as it is exact. Buy an alarm clock and an electric meat grinder and a scale that weighs in ounces.

"Stay up until eleven o'clock.

"Set the alarm for 7 A.M.

"Shave and dress in thirty minutes. Then eat and drink nothing that contains salt. You will have to stop all bread and milk and even meat. There is too much natural salt in meat to make it safe for you to try it until you have lost about fourteen pounds of dropsy. The edema that you call dropsy depends upon retained salt. When you get rid of more salt in your urine than you take in in your food, loss of the edema is automatic.

"Very seldom is really salt-free food prescribed. It is too monotonous and too tough. But I want you to have it. That means that you eat and drink nothing but lemonade, black coffee or clear tea with sugar, water, and raw or canned fruit. You can have as much as you want of any one of them; but that is all; and stay in the house, up and dressed during the daytime.

"Then, when I tell you that the edema is all out of your system, which should happen when your weight is around two hundred, your food will be completely changed, and you will start on this program:

"Leave the house at 7:30 A.M. to walk one minute away from the house and one minute back. Every day for twenty-eight days, try to walk thirty seconds farther away. But stop still if pain or breathlessness develops. Someone in the family or the chauffeur should trail you in the car. What you are trying to do is accommodate to a thirty-minute walk before breakfast, kept up, except in the case of snow or rain, for the rest of your life.

"Then come back to a breakfast which is exactly like lunch or dinner. The cook should cut off six ounces of lean chuck or top round or steak. All of the tough membrane should be cut off. Lean lamb or veal or pork or turkey or chicken can be used if that is preferred. The lean meat is then ground with two ounces of good white suet with parsley or celery leaves, a lot of pepper, and a little onion if you like it. The freshly ground meat is shaped into a thick cake and immediately fried or broiled.

"Make two portions at breakfast time. One should be allowed to cool, wrapped in aluminum foil or Saran Wrap, and taken with you for lunch. You are to stay out of restaurants for twenty-one weeks. You are too sick to be given any leeway in the amount of meat that you eat. I want a very exact quantity.

"With the meat, take only a medium-sized after-dinner cup of real clear strong black coffee. Between meals, drink six glasses of water, three in the morning and three in the afternoon.

"I shall want to see you for a checkup three times a week until the edema is all gone."

Mr. Thomas suddenly began to lose weight, and with it his edema, beginning on the third day. On the eleventh day he weighed two hundred and one pounds and was sleeping much better. The edema was apparently all gone and his food was changed to weighed freshly ground meat. The cook reserved a special fry pan for him so that no salty thing would be cooked in it. The patient seemed to prefer a great deal of pepper with his meat. He was given as much as he wanted.

At first, weight loss was rapid at seven pounds a week. Then it sharply dropped to three pounds and kept at that level. When he reached a weight of one hundred and sixty pounds he stuck there until it was discovered that he was drinking an extra demitasse while playing cards at night. Correcting that fault soon had him down to one hundred and fifty-four pounds. Then he was given four things with a meal with a prompt gain in weight. Back on his ground meat and demitasse, and he dropped to one hundred and forty-nine pounds. That proved to be a tolerant weight.

Time was when such patients as Mr. Thomas were put to bed and kept there until free from dropsy. Then it was found out that the cardiac clock had a tendency to stop permanently when all familiar activity was taken away. Now they are kept active.

Apparently the reason he was willing to follow such strict

orders was because I let him continue to smoke his beloved cigars. As long as he didn't take liquor, I didn't care much. Smoking does give some people angina, but seldom does one see such a case. And it is usually safe to trade tobacco for alcohol. A man is never completely lonely when he can smoke.

That talk I gave him about stairs seemed to have made an impression. He built a new house all on one plane, and level with the floor of his car. When he at last learned that the size of his heart was more important than the electrocardiogram, he stopped his practice of having one taken every two weeks.

When his weight became normal he was strong enough to play golf on an absolutely flat course, but he takes his morning walk religiously even if he is going to play golf afterward. I told him that stop-and-go exercise such as golf was nowhere near as good for him as steady walking.

About the only stairs he ever climbs are the ramps leading into airplanes. I told him to put two feet on each step of the ramp and to take a long time.

His life has apparently been prolonged and illustrates an important point in the treatment of heart disease. A Ford engine is no good in a Cadillac car, but a Ford engine, even when damaged a little, can run like the very devil when it powers a suitable body.

Business organizations think that they extend the life span and increase the efficiency of their employees by periodic health surveys, including chest X rays and electrocardiograms. Once in a great while they do pick up a case of previously unrecognized active tuberculosis that would be better off taken out of the running. As far as lung cancer is concerned it is almost always too late when there is positive X-ray evidence. The patient would be far better off continuing to work in ignorance of his condition.

Machine diagnosis is only a small part of the evidence considered by the skilled family physician. He knows that machines can tell lies and laboratory reports be in error. Plenty of people have been told to go home and put their affairs in order because of a loose string in the electrocardiographic machine or because the elevator in the building happened to be running close by. It is not generally understood that the main value of the EKG has been in research work. Thanks to its use we now have a much better understanding of altered rhythms in the heart. Most patients seem to think that an EKG can exactly predict the length of life, exactly where and to what extent a blood vessel in the heart is plugged up and when it becomes open again, and exactly what and how much medicine is indicated. All of which is stretching a long bow indeed, because a patient can suddenly die with a normal EKG report or live and work for a long time with a bad one.

The sheet anchor of the family physician is the size of the heart. If it is normal or small it can practically always be disregarded as a cause of trouble. A good fluoroscopic examination can demonstrate that instantly, and in about ninety-five per cent of cases in office practice the heart will be normal in size. A heart responds to interference with its own circulation by prompt enlargement, and the rule is that the bigger the heart the poorer it is.

When the coronary arteries become plugged, usually from extensive and severe hardening of the arteries, the outcome depends a great deal on where the block occurred. If it is in the wall of the heart it may be fairly silent and nature will seal in the damage with what looks like a milk patch. At autopsy as many as five or six of these old patches may be noted, with no record in the history of the patient of trouble in the region of the heart. But if a main trunk becomes stopped up it is a lot like the plumbing in a country house, when roots from the maple trees have worked in and clogged up the main pipe. Pouring an alkali down the toilet bowl or passing a plumber's snake through the pipe is not going to do any good. The pipe has to be dug up and replaced. And so it is with the present-day vogue for the administration of drugs that reduce the clotting ability of the blood. The patient survives if the damage is slight, and in the wall. He would recover anyhow. But death can seemingly be accelerated by the use or abuse of anticoagulants when a main trunk is in trouble. Much more research work is needed before these dangerous drugs can be evaluated. The last four cases for which I used anticoagulants did not live, so perhaps I am unduly pessimistic.

If you have real coronary trouble in a main branch, it is better to just go to bed and stay there for six weeks to give nature a chance.

Pneumonia used to be considered the final solution to the problems of the aged, but now coronary artery disease is the big killer after the age of fifty. All sorts of reasons have been given for the frequency with which it occurs. Obesity, a high intake of saturated and hydrogenated fats, luxury living, social and business stress and strain, physical indolence, alcohol, and tobacco have all come in for criticism, but there is proof of nothing.

Some considerations have been lost sight of in the mad race to live forever. An old saying among the Negroes is that "some folks just don't make old bones." That tendency may save you from some worse fate which nature might have in store for you. However, people can grow old gracefully. You do see hale and hearty and happy folks still usefully working after the age of eighty-five. But they are fearfully outnumbered by the ones with the inability or disinclination to work, and by failing vision, hearing, strength, sphincter control, digestion, and other handicaps. No! People don't usually become gentle and kindly and full of wisdom as they grow older. More commonly, I should say, they are irritable and malignant and dull. Never envy the aged. Life is a real battle to keep comfortable after the age of sixty-seven.

Everyone has an obligation to keep as young as possible. That implies useful work no matter how humble, and some serenity of mind, and normal weight, and daily outdoor exercise, and enough amino acids in fresh fat meat to do a good job of repair on breaking-down arteries.

And that is a big order. If it can be fulfilled a lot of other things can safely be left to nature. She was practicing medicine a long time before anyone heard of physicians.

Chapter VII

OSTEOARTHRITIS

OSTEOARTHRITIS is what is called a one hundred per cent disease. We all get varying amounts of it if we live long enough. That little swelling and deformity of the finger tips, or creaking knees, or lower-back pain may be the first signs of it. Interference with the circulation in the joints can start up promptly at the dangerous age of thirty-three when we all begin to get hardening of the arteries.

The earlier correct treatment is started the better, but there is still hope for a lot of sad people abandoned in wheel chairs. I dislike wheel chairs. With arthritis they can mean that both the doctor and the patient have quit fighting.

A patient who had survived an intestinal obstruction came in to see me about the possibility of helping a bedridden friend. The story she told was of an arthritic of ten years' standing, unable to get out of bed, and with a most obstinate constipation. Drugs to relieve pain had increased the constipation and the woman had been forced to resort to daily enemas.

This had resulted in bleeding hemorrhoids. The family was resigned to the permanently bedridden state but hoped something might be done about her intestinal tract. So I journeyed uptown to see the patient.

She proved to be an obese, pain-racked individual, fifty-eight years of age, cheerful and courteous in spite of all her misery. The family history revealed that one grandmother, late in life, had been bent almost double with arthritis. Her personal history was unimportant save for the fact that she had gained about forty-two pounds with her first pregnancy. She had had four children in all, and following each succeeding pregnancy it had been harder to lose weight. Her weight had remained fixed at one hundred and seventy-two pounds since the last child was born.

Pain in the knees on stair climbing came on one year after her periods stopped. Progressively, pain and stiffness involved the fingers, hips, back, feet, and shoulders. She had been treated at clinics in Boston and in Hot Springs and in Europe, but the condition had steadily become worse. Everyone had advised her to lose weight but it seemed impossible to lose. For her arthritis, she had tried supposedly radioactive mud in Germany and huckleberries in Czechoslovakia. Baking and massage were of no benefit.

Her present trouble followed directly after a nine-week stay in a hospital during which time she was confined entirely to her bed. Some teeth had been extracted and she had been given gold treatment, butazolidin, and intensive dosage with cortisone. The cortisone treatment had been discontinued when she developed swollen breasts and a moonface. She had been returned to her home by ambulance and instructed to continue with massage. Codeine had been prescribed for unbearable pain. Privately a member of the family informed me that they had been given a very unfavorable prognosis as to her arthritis, and that she could not expect to walk again.

Available for inspection were several series of X-ray pictures dating back ten years. These showed sharpening of the edges of the bones with deformities of the fingers, considerable destruction in the right hip, and bridging of the spinal vertebrae. Gall bladder X ray was negative for stones. There was no sign of intestinal obstruction.

Physical examination, aside from obesity, showed a small strong heart and good elastic arteries in the back of her eyes. None of her joints were completely frozen, though movement elicited pain and creaking sounds. The knees were swollen but there was no evidence of free fluid in the joints. There was no obstruction in the rectum and the hemorrhoids did not require surgery. It wasn't a good setup, but it wasn't too bad either. The woman impressed me as a fighter, if only she knew what to fight. I asked for a pad of paper and wrote:

"Dear Mrs. Emmet:
"You have a diagnosis of:
"1. Obesity. Your weight of one hundred and seventy-two pounds is forty-two pounds too much. . . . You will have to go down to your high school weight of one hundred and thirty pounds if this kind of arthritis is to be controlled.
"2. Osteoarthritis. Another name for it is menopause arthritis. It is much akin to the large bunions you have on each great toe joint. It is an inherited disease, starting up sometime after the age of thirty-three, with a particular likelihood of development after the menopause in anyone who is overweight. There is no tendency for the ends of the bones to grow together. The stiffness depends on the mechanical

changes in the structures around the joints. The pain is a good thing, and nature's way of telling you to get busy. Except for the liberal use of aspirin, and no other drug, you will have to try to disregard the pain and work on the function. All of these joints have to be stretched. Bones tend to soften, at times almost to the consistency of cheese, when you stay in bed. You will have to get out of that bed no matter how much it hurts. The bones must be kept hard by use. As soon as you can stand up well, a special exercise will be given you for each affected joint. These exercises have to be kept up thirty times, three times a day, perhaps for the rest of your life.

"Your bowels are not too weak. They are too strong. All you will need to get them going is proper food and patience. The hemorrhoids have to be washed with a soap-and-water lather three times a day. The first thing to do is stop using a bedpan and have a commode beside the bed. Use that for everything, no matter how excruciating the pain.

"Then I shall arrange to have a walker delivered at the house and you will have to practice standing in it. Expect to lose weight at the rate of seven pounds a month on three things with each meal. You are in for a fearful battle for the next six months. Follow this routine to the letter.

"Keep awake except for eight hours at night and a twenty-minute nap after lunch. You will have to arrange with the cook for an early breakfast, so that there will be five full hours between breakfast and lunch. To make progress you need a great amount of something called amino acids to build and repair the cells in your body, especially around the joints. Fresh fat meat is the best available source of amino acids, so I want you to get outside of a half pound with each meal. Usually a pan-broiled shell steak that weighs ten ounces and has a liberal rim of rather hard fat on the outside is the most palatable.

"Breakfast is the hardest meal to get used to, so get one of those new small stout electric grinders and a scale that weighs in ounces. The grinder costs around forty dollars and the scale twenty-three dollars. Have someone roast for you a leg of lamb and a three-rib roast of beef without salt. For each breakfast, cut off one half pound of the cooked lamb or beef with some of the fat. A freshly boiled potato is added to that along with pepper and fresh parsley and a thin slice of onion, and any other spice you like, but not salt.

"That combination is run through the grinder and reheated in a frying pan with a tight cover. Add a sherry glass of water before reheating. Properly done, it should be delicious, and you eat it for breakfast along with a demitasse of black coffee.

"With lunch and dinner, you can have any fresh fat meat you like providing that pork and veal are top grade. Corn-fed pork is the kind you try to get, along with prime beef and Kentucky lamb. They taste better, and are better for you than second-, third-, and fourth-grade meats. If you eat chops, have at least two double-rib Frenched chops with each meal. Club cuts of roast beef, one half inch thick, cold or hot, are good. Ground meat has to be ground at home and cooked within ten minutes of grinding. Grind six ounces of lean and two ounces of suet, parsley and pepper, and a little onion or chives if you like. Shape this into a cake and fry or broil it. Potatoes can be white or sweet, baked or boiled or home fried in melted suet. But no salt or butter can be used. The demitasse is to be of real coffee without sugar or saccharine. Between meals drink six tumblers of water. Stop your physiotherapy. Six months from now, which will be on the fifteenth of August, I want you to be in a size sixteen evening gown at a dinner dance."

This, from a medical standpoint, is what you might call going out on the end of a limb and sawing it off. But I had seen lots of worse cases than hers get better and I was gambling that Mrs. Emmet had spunk.

Her progress was fascinating to watch. When she announced, after seventy-two hours, that the pain in her joints was lessening and that she felt stronger, the family took heart and was most co-operative. Money was not a consideration, and they were delighted to do anything that might enable Mother to get back into circulation.

The walker was tried on the third day. Within a week Mrs. Emmet had the rugs taken up and was pushing the thing around the room. The family was getting really interested by this time, and a plumber and a carpenter were called in. Parallel one-inch pipes were erected thirty inches apart and at the level of the patient's hands. The tracks led directly to her bathroom and to the dining room. Hand supports were put in beside the toilet bowl and around a new walk-in shower bath. A rope was suspended firmly from the ceiling in front of the toilet bowl, so that she could pull herself to her feet. The parallel pipes braced into the beautiful dining-room floor led directly to her accustomed seat. No one was allowed to help her with anything. For with osteoarthritis, the game is to be completely independent.

Which is a little like the old tale they tell down in Arkansas.

After a terrific rainstorm, an automobile was trying to negotiate a country road. The driver spied an old felt hat moving along the top of the mud in a ditch beside the road. He stopped his car, walked over to the edge of the ditch, and cautiously lifted up the felt hat. Underneath was a colored man's head. The motorist inquired, "You got trouble, boy? You want some help?" The reply was, "No, sah! I got a good mule under me. We'll mek it."

When the patient had had no sign of a bowel movement after five days on the new food, she was given a full bottle of citrate of magnesia. And that was the last trouble she had with constipation. She was taught that primitive people with access to meat fat depend entirely on it to regulate bowel movements. In the far North, an Indian or Eskimo knows that by regulating his intake of caribou fat he can have as many bowel movements as he pleases. Civilization tends to make us forget the simple things. But the novice reducer has to be patient for the first couple of weeks. Three big meals, plenty of water between meals, and bodily exercise are also necessary.

Soap and water took care of the hemorrhoids. Mrs. Emmet was taught the cleanly habit of immediately washing with soap and water on the hand, and then blotting with paper towels after every bowel movement. This is a great trick in preventing the strangulation of hemorrhoids.

Mrs. Emmet could finish about one half of her meat portions the first three days and then appetite came with a rush. Before long she called back the plumber and the carpenter and had a handrail laid along the wall leading out to the kitchen. In that way she could get out to see what went on in the refrigerator and on the stove. The freezer was discarded and all meat was top quality and fresh. Some friends brought her potatoes from Prince Edward Island that had a wonderful flavor. A new accurate scale without wheels was installed in the bathroom and a daily written record of her weight was kept on a calendar.

The special exercises were started on the tenth day. These exercises, particularly the back swinging, seem to represent a tremendous advance in the treatment of arthritis.

I had learned the value of exercise in the hospital wards. Internes are mainly interested in dramatic things like the diagnosis of a cancer not connected with a hollow organ, while the visiting physician is perhaps more interested in getting someone back to work. So the resident would sigh when rounds were stopped beside some osteoarthritic abandoned in a wheel chair. The patient would be required to demonstrate the exercises that had been taught him, and it was all very time-consuming. But ninety days of exercise can work wonders.

Mrs. Emmet found out, as most patients do, that the exercises performed before breakfast were much more difficult than those before lunch and dinner. Eight hours in bed would stiffen her up a lot. But she kept at it and the family would cheer her on evenings by coming in with a yardstick to see how close her hands were getting to the floor. Ninety minutes after breakfast she would walk back and forth in her parallel bars, measuring the time with a watch, so that the time could be steadily increased.

It became advisable to spend more money. A special shoemaker, who knew how to make beautiful shoes that fitted toes as well as heels, was called in. Her feet were three and twelve-sixteenths of an inch straight across when the bunions were included. So the morning, afternoon, and evening shoes were all made that wide and with the kind of well-fitting heels that women like. The cost was great but for the first time in many years her feet were comfortable, and the shoes had style.

The next innovation was a door in the dining room and a ramp with parallel bars leading out to and around the garden. Mrs. Emmet had the interest and the time and a good gardener, and a perennial garden was laid out that was a wonder. A ramp was built with hand supports so that she could easily get into her car. By the fifth month she was driving herself, but weight loss, as she got down near the normal, began to slow up. So she was dropped back to the two things a meal, just fat meat and a demitasse. It was explained to her that she had to get to a tolerant weight. That probably would be one hundred and thirty pounds and with one and a half inches of loose fat between fingers on her lower abdomen. When she reached that point she would be tried on four things with a meal to see if her weight stayed normal. If she went up again she would be dropped back to one hundred and twenty-five and again tested.

But one hundred and thirty pounds proved to be adequate. Mrs. Emmet found she could eat fresh fat meat with a little salt, potato with butter, raw fruit, and coffee three times a day without gaining.

By that time she was really sailing ahead and the parallel bars leading to the dining room were removed. On her own accord she went to a studio for a refresher course in dancing.

Then her sons arranged a dinner party at a fine hotel with a good orchestra. Bent fingers, painful right hip, and all, but able to dance again, she was quite the queen. The only trouble was that in the shank of the evening she made a speech. She climbed to her feet and with great good humor commented on the vicissitudes of arthritis. "And after all that," she said, "Dr. Donaldson cured me with hash."

Which wasn't true, of course, but it didn't matter.

I was lucky with Mrs. Emmet. Not often do you get the chance to treat chronic disease in a patient with a cheerful heart, and an iron will, and more or less unlimited means.

But poor folks, inspired usually by the need to take care of someone else, can accomplish the same result. Even if you can't afford a meat grinder, you can still add six ounces of finely chopped suet to eighteen ounces of ground lean chuck and divide it into three cakes. It doesn't taste as good but it will be satisfactory. Beyond that it is a question of work and more work at the special indoor and general outdoor exercise.

Some of the trouble Mrs. Emmet had experienced in the hospital was due to the failure there to distinguish between osteo- and rheumatoid arthritis. The latter can respond temporarily to treatment with cortisone, with marked reduction in swelling and pain. But cortisone does not cure and can be dangerous. There was no indication for its use in this case. Osteoarthritis seems to be about twenty times more prevalent than rheumatoid arthritis, which is a wasting disease of younger people with a tendency to form rheumatic nodules and to have the inflamed membranes between the bones grow together in fibrous or bony ankylosis.

But even in true rheumatoid arthritis the treatment is little different once fever and redness have subsided. Aspirin is still the best and safest drug, and the exercises must be persisted in before bony ankylosis sets in. When that develops it is too late.

These exercises have proven, in my practice at least, to have sufficient importance to make it worth while to illustrate them with line drawings:

I

With the back of the hands locked so that you do *not* make a fist, close the end of the thumb and the ends of the fingers. You may not be able, especially at first, to touch the tips of the fingers to the palms. But keep at it. The exercise discourages something called Heberden's nodes in the terminal joints of the fingers.

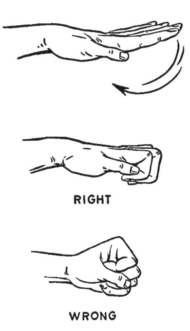

RIGHT

WRONG

II

With the elbows held firmly to the sides of the body, the wrists are rolled in a circular motion thirty times in one direction and thirty in the other.

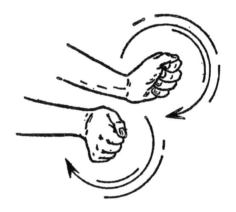

III

To free stiff elbow joints, with elbows held at the side and fists clenched, both forearms are punched straight out in front thirty times.

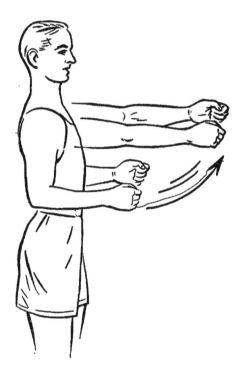

IV

To correct creaking and pain and stiffness in the shoulder joints, both arms are pinwheeled thirty times in one direction and thirty in the other. In this exercise the arms should describe as nearly perfect a circle as possible.

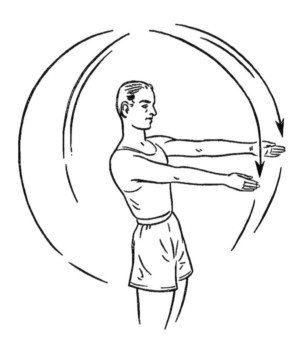

V

Now to attack that popular expression "Oh, my aching back!" This seems to be the most important of all the special exercises and there is a question as to whether or not practically all of us from the age of thirty-three on should perform this fifth exercise every morning on arising. A stiff lower back leads to the short steps that are a sign of old age, and the lower back is the first place most of us seem to grow old.

There are six distinct steps to the fifth exercise.

(1) Start with feet parallel and about two feet apart, knees held stiffly. Extend both arms straight up over head and hold the neck back as far as possible with each swing.

The eyes should be looking directly up at the ceiling. Come back to that position each time.

(2) Then, swinging forward from the small of the back, bring the arms down smoothly parallel with the floor.

Without pause or jerk or lunging or too sudden increase in effort, swing back to the starting position, 1.

(3) Swing down again, dropping the open hands two feet lower.

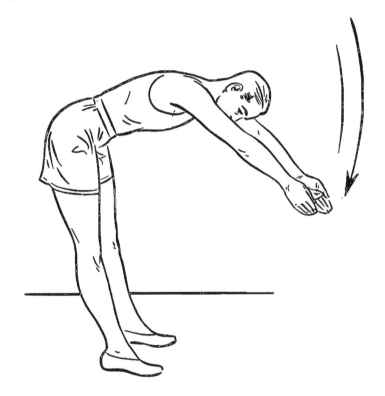

(4) Swing two feet lower.

(5) Clench the fists at the top of the swing and try to touch the floor in front of the toes easily with clenched fists. Keep the hands tightly clenched until this can be accomplished. But don't stay down, lunging to get lower. Go right down and right up again.

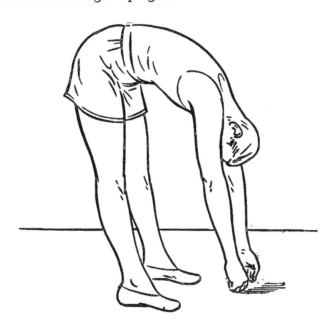

(6) After touching the floor with clenched fists and with knees stiff, open the hands and touch the floor with the tips of the fingers. Try to bring the heel of the palms nearer to the floor with each swing. When the backs of the palms touch with the whole palm on the floor, you have won the fight. Then as the exercise becomes easy and familiar, the palms should be placed on the floor twenty times.

It can take three days or three weeks or three months or three years before this can be accomplished. But keep it up.

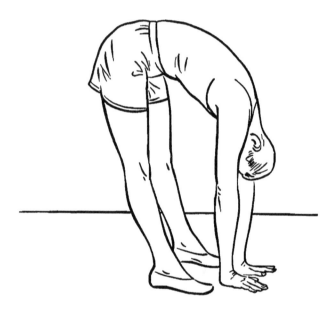

When the vertebrae in the spine are bridged by arthritis, it is usually necessary to continue this exercise thirty times, three times a day, for many years.

The ordinary painful, stiff lower back usually can be controlled by doing the exercise perfectly once a day on arising. But it must be done three times a day until such time as the goal of touching the back of the palms to the floor is reached. Cancer and tuberculosis of the spine, of course, have to be excluded before the exercise is attempted. But they are both great rarities.

Over the years many patients have come in bragging about sacroiliac slip, and herniated disc, and slipped disc, and spinal curvature as an explanation of their lower back pain.

Some of the patients have already undergone spinal fusion operations in the effort to correct this pain.

It is well to keep the fact in mind that X-ray pictures of the spine are just as different as are fingerprints. It is exceedingly difficult to tell what is normal and what is abnormal. An X ray of the spine can seem to prove almost anything that you want to believe.

So far I have had good fortune. All of the patients complaining of such conditions have had their symptoms completely, or almost completely, relieved by graded back swinging. Until such time as I find a patient who is not controlled by back swinging I expect to remain skeptical of such diagnosis as an explanation of lower-back pain. Hardening of the arteries in the muscles or joints, or else blood vessels that seem too small for the job of holding the back erect, seem to be a much better explanation, and these respond to correct treatment.

VI

To prevent arthritic feet:

With knees stiff, and holding onto two steady objects, rock up on the toes . . .

. . . and back on the heels thirty times.

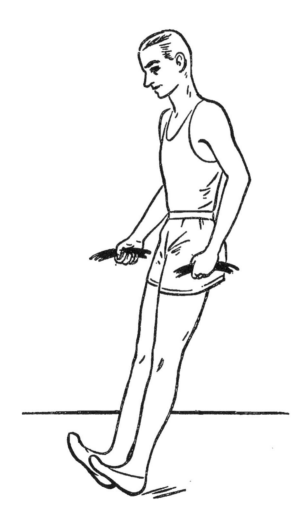

VII

For supple knee joints:

With hands on the hips or with both hands holding onto two steady objects (backs of two chairs will do), depending on the weakness of the knees, bend the knees thirty times.

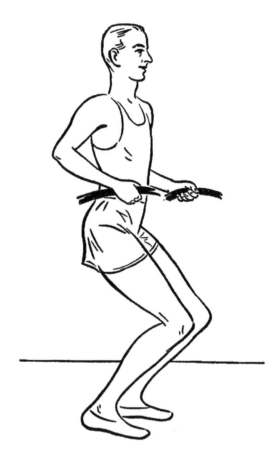

Chapter *VIII*

DIABETES

A STOUT WOMAN came hobbling into the office one morning, complaining bitterly of painful feet and cramps in the legs.

One grandparent had been much overweight and died with diabetes. Her mother was a diabetic and died of coronary thrombosis. The patient had been much overweight since her first pregnancy. At the age of thirty-three Mrs. Liebowitz suddenly began to get up frequently at night to pass urine. When her family physician told her she had diabetes she went to a specialist in that disorder. He put her on regular doses of insulin which stopped a great deal of the frequency of urination. Also, she had been advised to lose a lot of weight, but this she had never succeeded in doing.

The doctor taught her how to examine her urine for sugar. Every morning for twenty years she had religiously tested it. Gradually it had been necessary to increase the dose of insulin to keep the urine sugar-free. Now she was taking fifty units a day. When she reached the age of fifty, severe cramps in the legs would awaken her from a sound sleep. At the age of fifty-three, her feet began to give her pain day and night. She was worried about diabetic gangrene.

After her urine and blood sugar had been tested and an X ray taken of her legs and feet, she was examined.

Her color was good. There were some yellowish-brown patches on her eyelids which she disliked. Her dressed weight was one hundred and eighty-two pounds. Eye ground examination showed only moderate hardening of the arteries. Fluoroscopic examination of the chest showed, surprisingly enough, only slight enlargement of the heart, and moderate enlargement of the aorta. Two years before she had undergone gall bladder X ray with dye. That showed no evidence of stone. Good arterial pulsation was not felt in her ankles, but the feet were warm and not much discolored. She had big feet distorted with bunions and corns, and was wearing pumps.

The blood sugar report was 0.28 per cent with a small amount of sugar in the urine. Chalky deposits in the arteries in her legs were visible in the X-ray films.

All of these things were a pretty common setup and I told her this.

"Dear Mrs. Liebowitz:

"You have a diagnosis of:

"(1) Obesity. You should have gotten rid of forty-six pounds twenty years ago. But it is not too late.

"(2) Diabetes. One out of every three people who get twenty pounds overweight develop diabetes. If they inherit the tendency as you do, the percentage is one out of every two. The hope is that people will get a little bit smarter with each generation. Try to see that your own daughters are never allowed to go more than twelve pounds above normal weight with any pregnancy. That was where you got into trouble, and you don't want them to suffer in the same way.

"Diabetes is far more a mental disease than it is physical. Almost always, it is due to gluttony, and being told that you have diabetes doesn't change your desire for flour one iota. You can blame your own trouble on Danish pastry. It isn't nearly as funny as you think it is, when you succumb to the longing for it. For the thing that kills with diabetes is hardening of the arteries. And flour seems to promote hardening of the arteries more than any other single thing.

"Now just get this fixed in your mind:

"Flour includes whole wheat toast as well as white bread. Forbidden are gluten bread, protein bread, rye bread, crackers, Ry-Krisp, bran muffins, diabetic biscuits, waffles, pancakes, sandwiches, canapé on crackers, turkey and duck and chicken dressing, gravy thickened with flour, all pastry and cake, and pie crust.

"Stop those forever, if you want me to look after you.

"You are out of your mind when you take insulin in order to eat Danish pastry. Some good physicians are quite worried about insulin administration. They think that insulin itself may promote hardening of the arteries. And that is practically the whole danger in the diabetic state. There is little danger of going into diabetic coma nowadays. What you should worry about is a stroke or a coronary thrombosis or failure of circulation in your legs from excessive hardening of the arteries following diabetes.

"There are four classes of diabetics:

"(1) The total diabetic, who would more or less instantly die without insulin. Fortunately such cases are exceedingly rare.

"(2) The severe diabetic who has a regular insulin need to keep from losing weight.

"(3) The moderate diabetic. This is the common type to which you apparently belong. Most of the severe diabetics who need insulin show well-marked enlargement of the heart. You haven't got that, so I want you to see what happens when you stop taking insulin.

"(4) The mild diabetic. About all such people need to do is to get their weight normal by stopping flour, sugar, and alcohol.

"But because you have been taking a large amount of insulin (fifty units a day is a large amount), you will have to come into the office every day to be checked until I am sure it is safe to stop it completely.

"To gain strength as you lose weight, and not be hungry, is a real trick. You will have to eat a large amount of fresh fat meat three times a day in order to burn off your own fat. You will be allowed nothing with it but a demitasse of black coffee. When you are trying to lose weight at the rate of three pounds a week, respect your five mortal enemies: the failure to walk thirty minutes before breakfast, and flour, sugar, salt, and alcohol.

"Except for the liberal use of aspirin with each meal, and the wearing of shoes that are as wide as your feet, try to disregard the cramps in the legs and painful feet as much as possible. It should take at least ninety days to get comfortable. Every morning you will need to walk thirty minutes without stopping and three times a day you will have to swing your back and rock your feet thirty times. At the end of three months the blood supply will probably be increased to the point where you have much less trouble. Be patient and faithful. Every morning each foot has to be put on the bath stand and scrubbed with a brush and a good soap-and-water lather.

"Until you can get some shoes made, wear heavy boy's

Norwegian moccasins. And don't pay any attention to the shoe clerk's advice that they will chafe your feet.

"The yellow spots on your eyelids are called xanthoma. They follow diabetes. Leave them alone.

"Testing your urine every morning is much less important than you seem to think. Only one thing should matter. You probably have enough strength left in your pituitary gland and liver and pancreas to take care of a body that weighs one hundred and thirty-six pounds dressed. So stop fooling around and get down to that weight."

Then I gave her a detailed list of everything she had to do, exactly as in the treatment of simple obesity.

It will probably always be hard to get patients with diabetes to understand a great new principle. What they are fighting is arteriosclerosis and that has to be fought intelligently and courageously.

(1) There is to be no failure in the thirty-minute walk.

(2) Arteries must be repaired with a good weight of amino acids in fat meat.

(3) Body weight must be normal.

(4) Flour is never again to be eaten.

It isn't normal to live on milk and cream and cheese and ice cream and eggs and chocolate and wheat flour and alcohol. No! Man is a hunter. Most of the wheat flour should be fed to the animals. Let them go through the arduous labor of converting fodder into meat fat. And then eat the animal. That is the smart thing to do.

Mrs. Liebowitz, by the way, did well. She had no bowel movement by the fourth day and a dead-violet odor to her breath; so I gave her a couple of heaping teaspoons of epsom salts in a half glass of ice water, and instructed her to eat one half of a grapefruit with each meal for three days. After

that she went back successfully to her regular routine of
fat meat and a demitasse, which kept her blood sugar at a
high normal level.

Some member of the family walked with her at first to be
sure she kept going for thirty minutes. Within a week she
stopped complaining about the walk. For some reason or
other, broiled veal sausage made out of fat veal chops with
pepper and sage seemed to agree with her better than anything else. I didn't care as long as it weighed enough.
Operations for bunions are never desirable in the diabetic
state. She will never have decent feet. But at least she has
learned not to shut off their blood supply with narrow shoes,
and since she has been slopping around in big shoes, the
corns have disappeared.

The family disapproved the suggestion of having good-
looking morning and afternoon and evening shoes made for
her. Instead of that, some of them went off on a European
vacation. And that is pretty normal. The reason that some
people are wealthy is because they are mean-spirited.

She stayed home, and went clumping around in her Norwegian moccasins. When her weight got down to one hundred and thirty-six pounds she was tested for tolerance by
giving her four things with a meal. Instantly she went up
again so she was dropped back to two things with a meal
until her weight was reduced to one hundred and thirty
pounds. The second test for tolerance proved successful and
she has stayed at that weight. She is still somewhat bitter
about the huge amount of insulin she took for many years,
but glad to be out of that slavery.

I told her that she was not cured, and never would be.
But that she had learned to live without flour and therefore
would probably have a normal life span.

Cases like Mrs. Liebowitz's hit home pretty hard to

physicians. It doesn't matter how much a doctor knows about diabetes. If he can't get weight off and keep it off, he is useless to the patient. Doctors who have a tendency to be fat themselves and who have learned to control it seem to have a better appreciation of the problem.

The human body is a lot like an automobile engine. Leaving the choke out results in too rich a mixture for the good of the engine. Eating flour and sugar for most of us means that the choke is wide open.

Not all ordinary diabetics can trace their trouble to gluttony. Once in a great while, emotional stress can cause the miserable disease. I learned about that from an arrant coward who had never been fat. The night he got his draft notice, he had to get up three times to pass urine. In camp, he spent all of his time in the hospital. Within two weeks he was discharged as a severe diabetic. Three months later he died as a patient in the hospital with diabetic gangrene of the lung.

A boy and girl in love and under the emotional stress of courtship can finish a two-pound box of chocolates in an evening. That load of sugar, which does relieve nervous tension, can overwhelm a pancreas, and one of them may develop diabetes just from that one big box of candy. Fortunately such results are great rarities.

Flour and sugar are too rich for most of us, and are only important for those people who are thin or normal in their weight and do heavy manual labor.

There isn't much manual labor left, which is a pity, for perhaps nothing in this world tastes as good as a slice of fresh homemade bread with plenty of good butter.

Not too much severe diabetes is seen in my office. Most of the patients are classified as mild or moderate. They simply need treatment of the underlying arteriosclerosis with reduction of weight to normal and regular outdoor exercise. Little attention is paid to traces or small amounts of sugar in the urine. The blood sugar ninety minutes after a meal can be kept at a reasonable figure by controlling weight with primitive food. In my own experience only about four in a hundred of the insulin-taking diabetics seen in the office need to have insulin continued. The rest just require normal food and normal weight and hard outdoor exercise. The care of their feet is of great importance in the effort to prevent gangrene. Athlete's foot, and bunions steadily increasing in size, and corns and plantar warts, and dirt, all have to be guarded against by daily scrubbing and the insistence on much wider shoes. Like everything else in medicine, treatment should be as simple as possible.

Perhaps the newest thing in the treatment of severe and moderate diabetes is the way hunger between meals can be stopped. The patients carry with them a thick cooked lamb, veal, or pork chop. Regularly at 10 A.M., 3:30 P.M., and 9 P.M. a cold chop is eaten. Fat meat is completely satisfying because of the slow emptying time of the stomach after it is eaten. Every patient who has stopped taking unnecessary insulin is advised to do this.

Chapter IX

HARDENING
OF THE ARTERIES

Many years ago a stout middle-aged man paid a visit to the office. He was terrified of the nights. For two years, fearful cramps in the legs would develop after he had been asleep for two hours. Then he would limp into the bathroom and stand in hot water. The cramps would promptly recur when he lay down again. He had been advised to take large quantities of sleeping medicine for relief, with poor results. In the daytime, he was beginning to notice something called intermittent claudication. After walking about seven minutes, cramps in the legs would appear and he would have to stand stock-still for a couple of minutes until they passed off. Following examination, which included some X rays, this letter was dictated.

"Dear Mr. Appleton:
"You have a diagnosis of:
"(1) Obesity. Your correct body weight with coat and vest off should be one hundred and sixty pounds. One hundred

and eighty pounds is twenty pounds too much. Three months from today that extra weight should be eliminated.

"(2) Arteriosclerosis, involving mainly the arteries in your legs and the great blood vessel where it comes off the heart. The well-marked enlargement of the aorta called atheroma is not too serious if you will avoid great physical strain.

"But the beaded arteries in your legs, that show on X ray, require very exact treatment. The pain is caused by the accumulation in the tissues of a gas called carbon dioxide. There isn't enough incoming blood to wash it out. When it reaches a certain concentration pain develops. No one knows for certain whether retraining with rhythmic exercise increases the capacity of existing blood vessels or whether new ones grow. In any event, it usually takes ninety days to get free from pain. If the treatment fails, and there is some chance that it may, I would advise you to go down to the West Indies to live. You don't want to stay where your feet get cold in the wintertime. That makes things worse.

"While you are waiting, experiment yourself with electric blankets, deer hunter wool socks, and with three aspirin tablets taken in the middle of each meal. Stop your sleeping medicine. That just destroys your ability to fight. The whole battle for refreshing sleep is fought on the line of daily outdoor exercise. You have got to get back somehow to a thirty-minute walk without stopping. Now do this:

"If you are going to continue your custom of leaving for the office at eight o'clock, set an alarm clock for half past six. Don't try to compress time. It always should take you an hour and a half to get going.

"Any more than eight hours in bed at one time may increase hardening of the arteries, so don't attempt to go to bed until ten-thirty or later.

"On arising swing your back, with arms fully extended over

your head, in the exact way I demonstrated to you. The exercise pulls on the back of your legs. Right now your clenched fists are sixteen inches off the floor at the end of the thirtieth swing. The distance from the floor will be measured each time you come in the office. Eventually you will have to get the back of your palms on the floor, but to make progress the exercise will have to be performed thirty times, three times a day. Do it on arising, before lunch, and before dinner.

"Now as to your food:

"You are going to lose weight, while rebuilding the cells in your arteries with something called amino acids, so I want you to get at least one half pound of any fresh meat you like with each meal. Shell steak with fat on it, two double rib Frenched lamb chops, club cuts of roast beef one half inch thick, or home-ground chopped meat with suet in it seem the best. But the weight has to be there. You can use all the pepper and parsley you want, but no salt. The second item with each meal is a demitasse of clear black coffee or tea.

"The third is a choice. You can have either baked or boiled potato without butter, or a half grapefruit, a ripe pear, a freckled banana, or one third of a pound of grapes. Remember that I said a choice. If you fail to lose seven pounds a month smoothly on this food, you will be cut to two things with a meal, so be careful. Between meals drink exactly six glasses of water, three in the morning and three in the afternoon.

"Take a watch with you on the morning walk, which is done before breakfast. If it is raining or snowing, then go later in the day, though it is not as good.

"Walk six minutes the first day without stopping, winding up at home. The next day, try to do seven and so on up, increasing the walk at that time of day by one minute only. When you reach thirty minutes you have won your fight. Hold it there, but any time that pain develops, stop and wait till it passes off."

Mr. Appleton got along splendidly and was on schedule as to both weight reduction and relief of pain. That was partly because he was a good executive and had learned how to give and take orders.

Arteriosclerosis is probably the most efficient tool that nature employs in her effort to keep us from living too long, and in the main is perhaps not a disease but an aging process that can be within normal limits. Apparently there are dozens of factors that can seem to accelerate hardening of the arteries, but no one thing in particular that can be blamed. For instance, I have seen a baby at birth with arteries like clay pipes. Both the mother and the father of the baby had untreated active syphilis. You might deduce from such evidence that syphilis is a cause of hardening of the arteries. On the other hand I have seen hundreds of old syphylitics at the age of seventy or more with arteries as good as or better than average.

Nervous tension has received a great deal of blame for the frequency with which the coronary arteries in the heart become inelastic and occluded. Professional men and business executives who compete under conditions of stress and strain are prone to develop coronary thrombosis. Nature evidently picks as a winner the solid compact individual with a rather thick neck. Executive ability seems to go hand in hand with such a physical type. By the same token nature is fair. One who has more of one thing has less of another. Far too often such men at the age of forty or forty-five can be found stretched over their desks with a coronary attack.

They had fancied themselves too busy to take regular exercise and keep normal weight.

Mechanical injury to arterial walls from high blood pressure can be followed by extensive hardening of the arteries. Diabetes, and the comparatively rare diseases myxedema and nephrosis and xanthomatosis, can be followed by the same result. Death of a portion of the heart wall due to a plugged-up blood vessel is called myocardial infarction. That occurs fairly commonly in men but rarely in women below the age of forty, so there is apparently some endocrine factor involved.

Overweight is accompanied by a high mortality rate and while there is some, but no definite, proof that excess stored fat promotes chalky change, the inference seems almost unavoidable if the death rate is to be explained.

Lack of regular outdoor exercise has to be conceded as a probable cause of arteriosclerosis. The incidence of coronary artery disease is much lower among farmers, laborers, and rural groups than it is among city workers. A Negro in South Carolina or Georgia at the age of sixty-five seems far more likely to have fairly good arteries than one living in Harlem.

For many years research men have been looking for a single controllable factor in nutrition as a cause of hardening of the arteries. The work was perhaps started by the ancient prejudice against red meat. Fifty years ago nephritis, or Bright's disease, was commonly seen in the medical wards of hospitals. Perhaps because of the decrease in the use of lead carbonate paints it is seldom encountered nowadays.

Such people might have huge amounts of albumin in their urine, and marked hardening of the arteries. Because there is albumin in meat, the patients were promptly deprived of meat as an essential part of the treatment. Such treatment proved worthless, but the superstition that eating red meat produced Bright's disease and hardening of the arteries persisted. No one realized that in the old days people who ate meat wanted half a loaf of bread with it and that the bread could do more harm than the meat did good. Nowadays in the presence of kidney disease fresh fat meat is given to repair the kidneys and replace the loss of albumin.

Foodstuffs are members or derivatives of three classes of compounds: lipides, carbohydrates, and proteins.

Research men have put the brunt of the attack on a nutritional cause for hardening of the arteries on the lipides.

Lipides include (1) fats, (2) sterols and waxes, of which an alcohol called cholesterol is the most prominent member, (3) phospholipides, (4) glycolipides, and (5) hydrocarbons. Of particular interest are fats and cholesterol, and an antagonist of cholesterol called lecithin (a phospholipide). Lecithin can probably act like a detergent washing powder to keep cholesterol from precipitating out in the walls of the arteries. The reason for the particular interest in lipides is because fat droplets, consisting of neutral fats and crystalline plates of cholesterol and masses of cholesterol esters, can be found in the rotten material in worn-out arteries. Then, too, it has been proven that certain families tend to run high cholesterol levels in the blood and seem to be prone to attacks of coronary artery disease.

But cholesterol is an important constituent of all cells in the body. It or its esters form part of the framework of all living cells and it is closely related to a bile acid, a vitamin, a suprarenal hormone, a male sex hormone, and a female sex hormone. No one knows whether a moderately increased level of cholesterol in the blood is a good or a bad thing. It could be just a protection. No one seems to be benefited by living on a low-cholesterol diet consisting of rice and fruit.

As a matter of fact, those who have followed a low-cholesterol diet do not live any longer than those who don't.

Such a diet is lacking in the essential amino acids which are so necessary for the growth and repair of cells. Therefore interest in feeding or injecting experimental animals with substances that increase cholesterol levels is waning. There is no good laboratory animal to compare with the human body.

In the search for the possible nutritional cause of hardening of the arteries attention is now being turned to the quality of ingested fat. Saturated fats of either animal or vegetable origin raise the serum cholesterol levels. Some highly unsaturated fats (oils) from either marine or vegetable sources tend to lower it. But no one knows whether this is good or bad. Some excellent research on dietary fats is now being conducted in England. For those who are particularly interested, the work of Ahrens' is well worth studying.

One thing that has been observed in the study of quality of fat is that the Japanese and the Swedes, both of whom eat considerable quantities of fish, seem to be cancer prone. Fish oil is rich in unsaturated fat. In Japan, cancer of the stomach is the leading cause of death from cancer. In Sweden the death rate from cancer of white males at certain ages is two to three times as high as in the United States. But then again no one knows. The autopsy statistics may be faulty.

Suppose you, yourself, are accused of having a degree of hardening of the arteries increased beyond the point allowable for your years. What are you going to do about it, particularly if you have had a coronary attack?

I know what I would do. I would adhere strictly to the possible normal in eating if my weight happened to be correct. If I seemed to be overweight I would strive to lose, and if underweight I would strive to gain. Fresh fat meat without

1 E. H. Ahrens et al., "The influence of dietary fats on serum lipid levels in man," *Lancet*, 1 (May 11, 1957), 943–53.

salt, potatoes with butter, raw fruit, and black coffee three times a day would be the standard when the body weight is normal. The main consideration in feeding would be the repair of damaged arteries with the fresh fat meat.

Then I would try to get some elasticity back in my arteries with graded outdoor exercise taken on the level ground. The good things in life have to be earned.

The newest interest in the cause of hardening of the arteries concerns the rigid restriction on concentrated carbohydrate (flour and sugar) and the effect of regular exercise. The question is of great importance because all of us seem to start downhill at the age of thirty-three. Overweight seems to increase the tendency toward arteriosclerosis and cannot be controlled as long as flour and sugar are eaten.

It seems probable that the mental changes that take place after the age of thirty-three are more important to the individual and society than are the physical.

Ever since man stopped earning his living by hunting, undue respect has perhaps been accorded to the elders of the tribe. In the herdsman stage of our development older people still could be supported without undue strain on the family and tribal economy. At first they perhaps acted as historians to perpetuate tribal legends and then gradually took over the teaching of customs. Next, as they were allowed to survive while retaining wealth, they moved into positions of authority and strove to inculate the idea that white hairs meant wisdom. What evidence do we have as to the soundness of this idea?

One of the biological laws is that leaders rarely lead. They are pushed by remorseless pressure from behind, while they hold back desperately with heels and elbows in the attempt to keep things as they are. When things are left as they are the perquisites are not interfered with.

Most of us operate under an unchanging pattern. Sharply

at the age of thirty-three we begin to look for security. This longing is probably initiated by the physical changes that take place at that age. Most of us never get a really new idea after thirty-three. Courage and imagination steadily diminish, and we tend to move cautiously, in the effort to avoid giving any offense. Yet technical skills can be continually improved by experience. Indeed, in many respects older workers are more reliable and statisfactory to deal with than are the young.

Holding their own at the top of our swarming millions are such glorious exceptions as Winston Churchill, Herbert Hoover, Douglas MacArthur, and ex-President Eisenhower.

But think how few they are out of the many! Increasing maturity of judgment is seldom seen after the age of fifty-five. Older people tend to maintain authority by hanging on to their money. That quality alone is inadequate to head up great business organizations.

Someday we may be forced to try out a new system. No one over the age of forty-nine and without proved managerial experience would be allowed to start serving in a government office. At the end of a six-year term he could be retired at full salary. That is enough honor for any man, and he would still have time to work at something else for as long as his arteries held out. Only one in six hundred of us is supposed to have any particular degree of managerial sense. That quality is usually manifested early at the age of twenty-eight. Managerial sense is most commonly demonstrated by the ability to meet a good-sized payroll over a number of years. And my hat goes off to anyone who can do it. We would all probably be a lot better off if we restricted our agents in government to younger men drawn from that particular group.

As long as we live we need to keep working at something. Retirement means loss of importance, which is not good.

The progress of Mr. Appleton was watched with considerable interest over the years. Truly the place to learn something about medicine is in the office. It may take many years of observation before treatment can be properly evaluated. He did all right and became reasonably free from discomfort. Meanwhile I got to know him better.

For a great many years Mr. Appleton had familiarized himself with all phases of the operations in a big factory. Apparently he had a passion for detail and complete intolerance of errors by subordinates. He had become a sort of efficiency expert, with no one being groomed to replace him.

He went on and on until the age of eighty. Then Mama and the girls stepped in. They said it was a shame to let the old man kill himself with overwork. I was very dubious about that, but I did insist that he give up his beloved subway and go to work in a taxi. The expense of that griped him considerably.

So after five years more of work, and in spite of my objections, he quit. The womenfolks were delighted—for about forty-eight hours.

Prior to his quitting work, the household had run in an accustomed groove.

For sixty years Mr. Appleton had been launched at eight o'clock in the morning, to return home exhausted at six-thirty in the evening. Then there had been a highball and dinner, a little conversation, and bed.

For years he had nourished an idea that somehow or other he was being robbed, and that the household didn't run—it just happened. Two days spent in observing what went on at home confirmed his worst suspicions.

So with complete confidence he took on the women.

In some unexplained manner his whisky had been disappearing. He fired the servant and the cleaning woman who came once a week. All charge accounts were stopped and everything became cash on the barrelhead.

There was no more telephoning to the butcher. The newspapers were studied for loss leaders and the womenfolks began to push little carts. Toilet paper was bought by the carton instead of one roll at a time. A special gadget was purchased so that dry cleaning could be done at home. All laundry was labeled or stamped and checked two ways. No more could wet underthings wave in the bathroom or stockings be left there to soak. Personal clothing had to be washed in the basement.

Milk and cream smuggled into the icebox were poured down the sink. He had never realized how fat his wife and daughters were, and I had said overweight was bad. So into the garbage pail went the lovely baker's bread and peanut butter. Luncheon, instead of being catch-as-catch can from the icebox, became a dignified repast.

The shouts of happy grandchildren had echoed around the big house, but when they found out that a quarter could be earned only by doing two hours of useful work, they shunned the place as though it was stricken by the plague. In no time the once happy home was a shambles.

Because Mr. Appleton blamed his longevity on the advice he had received from me, my name became anathema in the household.

After a year of it I had another visitation from the wife and daughters. Wasn't there *some* way I could get the old man to go back to work again?

Chapter X

HIGH BLOOD PRESSURE

My SECRETARY informed me that she had blocked off an hour and a half for a V.I.P. The patient's office manager had called up to make the appointment, and said that it involved many reports and uninterrupted time would be needed. Mr. Unruh, who waddled into the office, proved to be the head of a large drug importing firm. Clutched in his hand was a briefcase loaded with all sorts of reports. His age was fifty-three and his chief complaint was of high blood pressure dating back for twenty years.

His grandparents and parents had been killed in various European wars. He knew little about them. His wife and four children were living and well. The personal history was unremarkable until he reached the age of thirty-three, when he began to gain weight. At the same time an elevated blood pressure of one hundred and seventy over ninety was noted. By the time he was forty years of age, both weight and the systolic blood pressure had increased to over two hundred.

From that time on he had spent a good deal of time in

various European spas and clinics in this country, trying to get his blood pressure reduced. Two sympathectomy operations in Boston had resulted in a drop of blood pressure for only a few weeks. He had been advised to have a third operation. At one clinic in the South, salt restriction had been so stressed that he was not allowed to lick stamps because of the salt in the mucilage. I knew something of what went on behind the scenes in that particular place, and asked him if the orderly had smuggled in any pickles. This he admitted.

Three or four places that specialized in medical surveys had presented him with sheaves of reports on cholesterol estimations and blood sugar curves and metabolism tests and electrocardiograms.

The man had really been around, and apparently took great pride in having access to all the latest drugs that had been introduced for reduction of blood pressure. These drugs he was taking faithfully.

In one clinic his weight had been reduced twelve pounds, but that was associated with a sense of weakness and he had quit. His present complaint was a feeling of apprehension and insomnia.

Physical examination showed an obese compact middle-aged man with a worried manner. He showed only moderate evidence of the hardening of the arteries that so commonly follows obesity and high blood pressure. The arteries in the back of his eyes were slightly shrunken but kidney function seemed good. The fluoroscope showed only a moderate bulge to his aorta and the heart showed only the beginning of enlargement. The blood pressure reading was two hundred and thirty-six over one hundred and four.

It wasn't a bad setup and I summoned the secretary for dictation.

"Dear Mr. Unruh:

"You have a diagnosis today of:

"(1) Obesity. Your weight of two hundred and twelve pounds is forty-eight pounds too much. Your goal is to reach normal weight at one hundred and sixty-four pounds, with coat and vest off, sixteen weeks from today.

"(2) Arterial hypertension. Your systolic blood pressure fluctuates between two hundred and forty-four and two hundred and thirty-two. The diastolic blood pressure is relatively low at one hundred and four.

"I don't know whether this is true high blood pressure or not. About one third of the people with this kind of elevated blood pressure have it return to normal when weight is reduced to normal by good food and exercise. Then the condition is labeled false high blood pressure. Another third show a considerable reduction in blood pressure, possible to around one hundred and eighty systolic, as weight returns to normal.

"The last third show no reduction whatever with weight loss. The systolic pressure remains at the same high level and can suddenly increase fifty points with any emotional stress.

"The first thing you should do is to find out which group you belong in. One thing has impressed me about you. Medicine is an art as well as a science. And it strikes me that you need a lot more art and a lot less of the half-baked science you have been subjected to. Nothing is going to help you but reduction in weight, and in twenty years of effort you haven't even made a start.

"Your idea of submitting to a third sympathectomy operation is, I think, most ill advised. You were operated on in the first place for scotch whisky and rye bread, so why have another operation?

"When your weight is reduced to normal, you may have

sufficient tolerance to be able to take one two-ounce drink of whisky before dinner. You will have to try it and see what happens. But alcohol is completely out of the picture until your weight is normal, and flour in all forms has to be eliminated forever. Bread isn't the staff of life in these times. Rather it is the staff of death.

"You are too sick to fool around with drugs. I know of no drug that has any real importance in the treatment of this kind of high blood pressure.

"What you don't understand is that most of the research work is done on worn-out hospital cases with fixed high blood pressures and what are called irreversible changes. You are not in that category at all. Apparently, you are just a careless eater and drinker, and following the high blood pressure you are drifting into something called anxiety state. That condition makes you a natural-born sucker for every drug that comes along. Try to get a little skeptical, throw your medicine away, and get interested in the prevention of hardening of the arteries. That is what kills with high blood pressure and you don't want to die.

"You will do better working than you will loafing with high blood pressure, so go to work.

"You are allowed only eight hours in bed out of the twenty-four, whether you sleep or not. Allot ninety minutes to get going, and time that with an alarm clock. Gradually train yourself to be in deep sleep when the clock goes off. There is nothing that is much good for sleeplessness but a thirty-minute walk before breakfast. Usually you'll find that after you have done that morning walk five times, you will sleep deeply on the fifth night. Allow thirty minutes to shave and dress and to swing your back, thirty minutes to walk and thirty minutes to eat.

"You are going to burn your own fat off in the flame of

fresh fat meat. Get a scale and find out what a correct meat portion looks like, beside the bone, and after cooking. You can have any meat you like, but I think you will find that a pan-broiled shell steak tastes the best. It doesn't matter whether it is rare or well done as long as at least two ounces of fat are left on it after cooking. You can have more than a half pound if you want it, but no less. You are depending on the fat to have regular bowel movements after the second week. Use whatever freshly ground pepper and chopped parsley you want, but no salt. And don't dot the steak with butter.

"Take nothing with the meat but a demitasse of real coffee without cream or sugar or saccharine. You should be free from hunger on this food. In restaurants for lunch, try always to get a club cut one half inch thick of cold or hot roast beef. That should be reasonably free from extra salt.

"Between meals, get a measured amount of water, exactly six glasses, three between breakfast and lunch, and three between lunch and dinner."

Mr. Unruh was lucky. As a matter of fact, the relatively low diastolic pressure suggested at the time that he might be. The blood pressure dropped sixty points with the loss in the first week of six pounds. That pleased him no end, and with a sort of Teutonic efficiency, he really went to town. The family called me up in despair over the smoke in the kitchen, but I just told them to paint the walls oftener, and if they wanted to, put a big hood and exhaust fan over the stove. For luncheon, he took a taxicab to the restaurant in town that served the best roast beef. Even from the start, he was free from nausea. I had told him that the theater was the only thing good for nervousness, so instead of collapsing over the evening paper at night, he began to step out. Some of his office staff were commandeered for bridge and poker games and then he began to check up on his country-wide business connections. That meant a lot of air travel, and he had to solve some difficulties in securing proper food. A thermos bucket fixed that problem, but even that wasn't easy. One day he told me about it.

"You know, Doctor," he said, "it's a funny thing. My family thinks the world and all of me. They would do anything for me except something practical. Do you think I can get anyone to take that thermos pail to the butcher and have it packed with eight choice shell steaks each wrapped in Saran? Not by a damn sight I can't. I have to do it myself."

And that is the way of it, of course. If you want anything done perfectly, you had better do it yourself.

The sleeping took care of itself, as I had told him it would. He planned his trips so that there was no night travel, and he could always get in his morning walk. It was a real victory when he told his wife to clean out the medicine cabinet, lock, stock, and barrel. The nervousness has persisted, but a full and useful life pretty well takes care of that.

His weight loss was only one week behind schedule, and that was due to a head cold. I put him on four things with a meal for a week when that developed.

At the seventeenth week he weighed one hundred and sixty-four pounds and had a blood pressure steadily ranging around one hundred and twenty-eight over eighty. Apparently he has many useful years ahead of him.

The anxiety state that commonly follows high blood pressure can be a most annoying thing. The victims feel as though a sword is suspended over their heads and they never seem able to draw a peaceful breath.

A busy medical office can't handle more than twelve people with anxiety state at one time. The neuropsychiatrists can get relief by shutting off their phones at night, but as a medical man can't do that, certain patients are likely to call you in the middle of the night to tell you they haven't eliminated since half past two that afternoon. This sort of news gets monotonous.

There seems to be nothing that relieves anxiety state but hard outdoor exercise and useful work.

Hard work is wonderful medicine.

Chapter XI

GALLSTONES

THERE is no question about it. If a woman is fat, fair, and forty, and has borne some children, she is the type most likely to be full of gallstones. Bile probably stagnates with both obesity and pregnancy. But always there is a tendency to forget ordinary explanations of trouble. Attention is focused on more dramatic things.

A fat woman was referred to me in the hope that I could stop recurrent heart attacks.

Like a good many patients, Mrs. Morrison came in with a previous diagnosis of coronary thrombosis. She had no recollection of her grandparents but her father and two sisters were stout and subject to digestive disturbances. No one in the family had ever been jaundiced.

She had been overweight all her life and went up to one hundred and seventy-eight pounds with her first pregnancy. The weight remained about at that level. With each of her three subsequent pregnancies attacks of belching gas, nausea, and epigastric distress had been a feature. She had been short of breath on stair climbing ever since her first pregnancy. Her present trouble dated back four years to when she was fifty-two years of age. Suddenly, in the middle of the night, she was awakened from a sound sleep with a tearing knifelike pain over her heart. She vomited profusely. The pain was so agonizing in character that she distinctly remembered thrashing all over the bed. Her physician was called and put a nitroglycerine tablet on her tongue. In about three minutes the pain subsided a good deal, and he called a heart specialist in consultation. The portable electrocardiograph was called into play and supposedly revealed evidence of coronary thrombosis. She was given sedation and transported to a hospital in an ambulance. There she was kept in an oxygen tent for twenty-four hours and then kept in bed for nine weeks. At the end of that time she was allowed toilet privileges. She had received intensive dosage throughout of a medicine which was designed to prevent blood from clotting. Many laboratory tests had been made to be sure that the medicine was kept at a proper level in the blood. Since the return to her home she had led a very quiet life, avoiding all forms of exercise and especially stair climbing. This had resulted in an increased gain in weight and she now weighed one hundred and ninety pounds. For the frequent attacks of epigastric distress which she still experienced, she took nitroglycerine tablets with considerable relief.

It seemed to me there was something fishy about the story. When a main blood vessel gets plugged up in the heart, there should be a tendency to lie in a deathlike quiet to put the heart as much at rest as possible. Mrs. Morrison had thrown herself around on the bed. Nitroglycerine can help any kind of a spasm, and relief of pain with its use was no proof that the pain was cardiac in origin. An electrocardiogram can be in error and give the same appearance as severe heart damage. The use of oxygen doesn't mean much of anything. If Mrs. Morrison had had a real coronary, she would probably have been dead in three years after its occurrence. She had lived four years since her attack.

On physical examination, the woman's heart seemed good. The fast heart rate could have been caused entirely by apprehension. Some deep tenderness was elicited over her liver. Fluoroscopic examination was surprising. The heart showed no evidence of enlargement whatever.

Based on these findings, she was told that there was no evidence of heart disease and she would have to have a gall bladder dye test before the diagnosis could be established. X-ray examination showed a large gall bladder filled with hundreds of small stones.

The family raised the devil. All of the sympathy lavished on the patient as a cardiac had been wasted, and how could I guarantee that she would stand surgery? I told them I couldn't guarantee anything in medicine, but that anyone with a small heart who could walk into a doctor's office could probably take modern surgery in her stride.

The patient eventually decided the problem for herself after I told her that she should be able to drive her own car twenty-two weeks after she was operated. It would take that long to get her weight normal.

The surgery didn't bother her at all, although it did take two strong orderlies to get her out of bed. The anesthetist reported that her heart rate speeded up just at the time the surgeon was removing the gall bladder, but that is a normal reaction. There is likely to be a reflex action on the heart when anything happens to the gall bladder. Her convalescence was uneventful.

The original mistake had been made in trusting the electrocardiogram rather than a plate of the heart taken at a distance of six feet. Organic heart disease is practically always associated with enlargement of the heart. She should have had a gall bladder dye test right after her first pregnancy.

As soon as Mrs. Morrison returned from the hospital I put her on the simple obesity routine. Again the family raised the devil. What did I mean by putting anyone who had just had a gall bladder removed on a high meat-fat intake? That was crazy!

So they were told that, as far as I was concerned, the need to keep patients who did have or had had gall bladder disease on a low-fat diet was just an old wives' tale. Even when gallstones were present, a patient got along better on fresh fat meat three times a day than on anything else. But it was entirely possible that she might have distress for a few days until used to the new routine. Fortunately, I was spared that with Mrs. Morrison. She took to her two double rib Frenched lamb chops three times a day like a duck to water. It only took ten days to get her up to the thirty-minute walk before breakfast.

She commented, as many do, on the sudden development of a feeling of well-being after she had been on the new food for three days. That should be due to the increased intake of amino acids, but no one knows for sure.

I don't believe I have ever had better co-operation from a patient. Her weight came right down to normal and stayed there when she was tested for tolerance. She was so relieved to be over the dread of a heart attack that she was willing to do anything.

One thing has to be kept in mind when gallstones show up in the routine examination of a patient suffering from indigestion. The gallstones may be completely symptom-free, and the belching of gas and distress due only to errors in living. Taking a gall bladder out, even though it is full of stones, won't help that. And the patient is no more comfortable after surgery than before. It is well to put such patients on a good routine first to see what happens. If that makes them entirely comfortable, that may be all there is to it. The gallstones can occasionally be left alone without too much danger to the patient.

But if the belching of gas, or distress, or attacks of vomiting, or fever, or pain in the back of the head continue, or jaundice develops, you can't call in an experienced abdominal surgeon fast enough. In such a case, it isn't desirable to fool around with medical treatment. If a patient can climb a flight of stairs without undue distress, it is entirely probable that he or she can stand good surgery, and you don't want to wait until a small stone moves into the common duct and gives rise to jaundice. That also can give rise to severe pain. Painless jaundice may be due to ordinary infectious hepatitis, but also, and especially in elderly people, it can be due to an extremely serious disease of the pancreas. So you can be grateful for severe pain when the white part of your eyes turns yellow. Painful jaundice is easier to correct than is the painless kind.

The gall bladder is only a reservoir where bile is concentrated and expelled in a proper relationship to meals. By the time it gets full of stones, it is dead for all practical purposes. The ducts in the liver have usually dilated enough to take on its function.

But the common duct is holy ground. That is usually the single connection between the most important organ of all, which is the liver, and the small bowel. Any trouble in the common duct can give rise to violent symptoms, because the lumen in it is not much bigger than the lead in a pencil. To open and probe it, and if necessary extract a small stone, requires great surgical skill. Because that has to be followed by prolonged drainage it increases the length of the post-operative care. If possible, it is always desirable to move in before the common duct gets involved.

John Erdmann was perhaps the most experienced gall bladder surgeon of all time. He was an extremely forthright man. One day I happened to be in a room where he was doing a dressing. The woman patient looked up at him and asked, "Dr. Erdmann, will this scar show?"

"That all depends," said the boss.

Chapter XII

ALLERGY

My PARTICULAR interest in the subject of allergy began in 1919 when I was running the diagnostic clinic and teaching graduate students at the New York Post Graduate Medical School and Hospital.

The students enjoyed nothing better than to catch the teacher in error. One day they asked me what I thought of the research going on in the arthritis clinic. The men engaged in that work had abandoned as useless injections of boiled milk put up in ampoules for the convenience of administration. Now they were injecting freshly boiled milk into patients with inflamed joints. Some of the apparently favorable results obtained were difficult to explain.

I looked dubious and told the students that I thought it just one more of the unimportant treatments that are "accorded with emphasis." What that means, of course, is that a certain percentage of disease processes are self-limited and get well in spite of treatment. The last thing done seems to cure even though it had nothing to do with the outcome.

Perhaps twenty per cent of disease processes fall into such a category. A physician with few qualifications except sales-manship could carry on with that percentage of improve-ment, especially if a dramatic thing like a hypodermic in-jection had been used. A real physician despises an emphatic treatment which is not directed toward the cause of a disease. And having delivered my homily, I suggested that we try the idea out. After a bit of search in the clinic outside of the amphitheater I came in with two patients. They both com-plained of joint trouble.

One was an elderly fat man with hugely swollen knees containing deposits of something that looked on X ray like chalky sponges. He had a diagnosis of villous arthritis. Stair climbing was an agonizing performance, and his condition fitted the picture of a severe chronic disease process that should not be affected by an "emphatic" treatment.

The other patient was a woman with an immensely swollen right ankle with a red blush over it. When quizzed as to the probable diagnosis, the students variously suggested that she might have phlebitis or arthritis or gout. Then I pointed out that all of such conditions are painful and she was walking around the amphitheater without discomfort, so that the diagnosis might be hysteria. Her history revealed that she had just witnessed her best friend being run over by a Second Avenue trolley car. The stump of her friend's ampu-tated leg had stuck up in the air and blood had spurted to the roof of the car. Within a few hours the patient's own right ankle had become markedly swollen and red.

Twice in my medical lifetime I have seen such a major hysteria. This was one of the times. It seemed obvious that any treatment, the more dramatic and emphatic the better, would help the woman in her trouble.

So both of the patients were injected with freshly boiled

milk and told to return on the following week for a checkup.

To my embarrassment, and to the students' unholy joy, they were both much improved. Obviously, some underlying allergic process had been affected in the man with swollen knees. There and then I decided that I had better learn something about allergy.

Not too much was known about it then, nor, for that matter, is it now. The efforts of dedicated research men to throw some light on the way that the bodies of many of us resent new things have resulted in a confusing new terminology. It seems to be so that any effort made by physicians to employ these new words in prescribing treatment discourages patients. Simplicity is the desirable thing if cooperation is to be expected. It is quite correct for a physician to debate in his own mind the difference, if any, between altered reaction, atopy, idiosyncrasy, sensitization, and anaphylaxis, but in office practice it is a good idea to sedulously avoid such descriptive terms. Things are tough enough for the little woman, with a number of allergic children, without bothering her with a lot of words.

The word "allergy" means a failure to get used to new things. A desirable state in any life would be the ability to eat and drink and touch and breathe in new things without reacting in an unusual and frequently unfortunate way. Only perhaps one third of us can do that. The other two thirds can do with a little prayerful consideration.

Sixty-five per cent of the patients who have entered my office in the past forty years have been diagnosed as having one or many of the sixty or so common manifestations of allergy.

Allergy is probably a recessive trait, like the white feathers on a Long Island duck.

Just as in many other things in life, the correct answer

to the problem of allergy is to marry away from it. Important dominant traits like responsibility for action in a man and charm in a woman need to be enhanced, while recessive traits or weaknesses, such as the inability to accommodate to new things called allergy, need to be bred out.

This is a lot easier said than done. Because once a boy and girl fall in love it can be expected that judgment will be suspended and imperfections entirely ignored. When two people, each suffering from some allergic disorders, have committed matrimony the road can be long and beset with expensive pitfalls. Everything comes out in the wash of matrimony: vision defects, teeth that need straightening, behavior problems, the inability to earn a living, allergies, and all the rest of the troubles. Only the amateur joy makers like the social workers think that environment amounts to much. They might rate it as ninety-five per cent, with heredity only accorded five per cent in the control of our lives. Whereas most well-trained physicians would just about reverse those figures.

On occasion one encounters youngsters who obviously possess two important talents. An open mind is coupled with leadership qualities. The world we live in today seems to be in dire need of such people. The responsibility of a physician is to keep them healthy and to try to guide them so that they won't be harassed with the support of a sickly family when they marry.

And that is what this discussion is about: how to recognize and avoid and treat allergic disorders, in the comparatively poor state of our present knowledge of the subject.

It could be called the biological approach.

The reason that allergy, even nowadays, is so seldom diagnosed seems to lie in the inability of many physicians to question a patient correctly. Early training helped me in that. Attending physicians like Harlow Brooks and Evan Evans at City Hospital had no use whatever for sloppy history taking.

More or less immediately after my experience with the man with swollen knee joints I happened to be stuck with the care of a number of children covered with that classic allergic disorder, generalized eczema. Eczema has long roots. As I began to go into the ramifications of the personal and family histories of these patients a little light began to dawn on the problem. I was particularly fortunate in finding a couple of the children with four living available intelligent grandparents. Of course grandparents control in heredity, and are of primary concern.

Long lists of the disorders the brothers and sisters, parents, uncles and aunts and grandparents had suffered with were made. Eventually a great underlying pattern seemed to appear. What apparently the grandparents transmitted to their grandchildren is something called shock tissue, which can affect any system in the body.

About sixty of what seemed to me the most common manifestations of inherited shock tissue were selected and from then on patients were continually questioned about them. As this went on, instead of thinking of allergy as a narrow field limited mainly to asthma and hay fever and eczema and hives, the picture got broader and broader.

Early skepticism about skin testing for offending substances helped. Skin testing was and still is important in certain cases of asthma and hay fever and contact dermatitis, but those conditions are only a small part of the big field. Some obviously allergic patients suffering from migraine and sinus trouble and eczema, and blessed with money and time to spare and scientific interest, helped to confirm my opinion of skin testing for offending substances. The patients allowed themselves to be injected with properly prepared extracts of different substances in the amount of many hundreds, for eight hours a day five days a week for two weeks. A record was kept of each reaction. After an interval of two weeks the same agents were injected in the same manner. In most cases the results were completely different. That wasn't any help to me and I looked for some different approach.

By this time I had become interested in feeding primitive food to patients with obesity. Halsey's dictum—"No one knows what is normal"—came to mind, along with the idea that perhaps no disease process requires a diet for prevention or correction. Some combination of normal food, whatever normal is, might be the correct way to feed people suffering from allergic disorders.

Some groups of children covered with long-standing generalized eczema were put under treatment in the effort to find a combination of food that would permit the whole group to recover. An almost endless amount of trial-and-error work seemed to show that three meals a day of fresh fat meat and potatoes and canned fruit, and all of the raw fruits except oranges and apples and strawberries and tomatoes and peaches, and black coffee or clear tea was the best combination. Any effort to feed milk or cream or cheese or ice cream or eggs or chocolate or wheat flour resulted in disaster to all or some members of the group.

The results after a couple of years' effort seemed to me sufficiently encouraging in generalized eczema to apply the same principles in feeding patients with other manifestations of the allergic state. For thirty-eight years the work has gone on and I have gradually developed the conviction that many baffling common disorders yield to such treatment. Things like postnasal drip and snoring and headaches and the sense of utter exhaustion which may be some form of internal hives can respond in a manner that is a source of vast satisfaction to both the patient and the physician.

Careful history taking is of great importance. Apparently there is nothing remarkable about one grandparent with eczema being responsible for a grandchild with shingles, another with duodenal ulcer, and a third with tremendous susceptibility to pneumonia. The shock tissue that is transmitted can involve the three great systems in the body: the skin, the mucous membranes, and the blood vessels. Or the shock tissue may be shown as a lack of virus and bacterial resistance, or else what is called physical allergy may be apparent.

There are perhaps hundreds of other allergic manifestations that are not on the list I ask patients about, but I am concerned with the things that are commonly seen in the office:

Vulnerable Skin: There is a question as to whether or not most skin diseases occur only as a manifestation of an underlying allergic state. It seems fairly certain that dandruff, acne, blackheads, boils, athlete's foot, contact dermatitis, marked poison ivy susceptibility, eczema, psoriasis, and drug rashes can be considered as such. A heavy body odor is usually in this class.

Vulnerable Mucous Membranes: Styes, canker sores, coated tongue, snoring, sneezing, heavy breath, postnasal drip, burning tongue, frequent colds, asthma, hay fever, gastric and duodenal ulcer, appendicitis, leucorrhea, gastric, and intestinal irritability.

Vulnerable Blood Vessels: Croup, sense of exhaustion, hives in three forms (ordinary urticaria, puffs under eyes, and puffy ankles); neuritic pain, certain alterations of blood pressure, shingles, painful menstrual periods, sudden redness of an eye, migraine, tic douloureux, lumbago, a type of dizziness known as cerebellar angiospasm, and Bell's palsy.

Bacterial and Virus Allergy: Pneumonia, scarlet fever, rheumatic fever, running ears, mastoiditis, growing pains, quinsy, chorea, tuberculosis, diphtheria, and probably, because four diseases seem to occur mainly in milk drinkers, it is safe to add infantile paralysis, sleeping sickness, glandular fever, and infectious hepatitis. It is unknown whether infection is milk-borne or whether the peptone in milk lowers resistance to infection.

Physical Allergy: Marked susceptibility to heat or cold or high humidity.

After several years of practice, with obesity and allergy as interesting side lines, I ran into something I didn't expect. One of the directors of the hospital asked me to come down to his office. The burden of his song was this: "You've been trained in diagnosis and you like to teach. You have some reputation among the surgeons for locating undrained pus. Why in the devil do you want to fool around with a lot of fat liars and nervous wrecks you call allergics? You've got the hospital superintendent half out of his mind ordering one half pound of meat three times a day for patients. No hospital in the world can afford that. Why don't you pull up your socks?"

The criticism was brutal but honest and meant in a kindly spirit for my own benefit. I thanked him and walked back up Lexington Avenue to the office thinking it over.

Of course in medicine, if you have enough private practice to carry on with, you are the willing slave of everyone in general but of no one in particular. I had enough private practice and decided to follow my stars wherever they might lead.

You never know what will happen in this world. Nowadays

potent drugs have changed the whole picture of infections. Consultation work is reduced to a minimum and at long last both the doctors and the public are becoming interested in obesity and allergy.

It is only in the last eight thousand years that we have had to accommodate rapidly to new things. Prior to that most of our dwelling places were located close to good water and where good hunting was available in the forests. Grasses and grasslands were few and far between until we began to clear away the trees. Probably there was little if any hay fever or asthma to plague us. Such disorders might interfere with the ability to smell out an enemy. All of the special senses had to be acute in those days if one was to survive, for the Spartan law was followed with a vengeance. Life went on in an orderly pattern for hundreds of thousands of years and little that was new was encountered.

Came the day, perhaps back on some paleolithic beach where the boys were digging for clams, when a hunter came dragging back a nursing animal that had been captured alive. On a bet some brave soul may have milked the animal and drunk a bit of the product. Inspired by that, they all took a chance, even though instinct should have warned them that a foreign substance would be floating in their blood streams. Perhaps two out of three of them promptly got sick with diarrhea or headache or skin trouble. Nowadays we call that allergy. Because it may take a million years before everyone adapts to a new thing, it can be expected that two out of three of us, especially after only eight thousand years of trial, will still react to an offending substance in the same miserable way. It seems a good rule to always put the blame on the forefathers.

Perhaps one of the things that has delayed progress in the treatment of allergy has been the concentration by research men on the problem of hay fever and asthma. Frequently in these two disorders it is possible to prove that some specific plant dust like grass or ragweed pollen is the chief offender. Dropping a solution of the extract from such a substance on the mucous membrane of the eye can cause a sharp inflammation. Scratch tests and patch tests and hypodermic injections into the skin can give rise to similar evidence of irritation, usually in the form of a hive. But even in hay fever and asthma such tests are not routinely reliable, and treatment by injecting carefully graded dilute solutions of the offending extract is not routinely successful. The work in this field is so fraught with difficulties that observers have not cared to venture forth into the common world of headaches and bad breath and sense of exhaustion and indigestion and eczema where skin testing for irritants has been proven to have little value.

There is perhaps no more educative experience for a young medical man than to be stuck with the care of a number of youngsters suffering with generalized eczema for three or more years. That is particularly true if the parents have been the rounds of some competent pediatricians and skin specialists without obtaining relief. Commonly such youngsters may only get amelioration of the intense itching by saturation of the skin with olive oil. The olive oil can become rancid, so that the patients smell to heaven. Eyes crusted with eczema can look like the proverbial burnt holes in a blanket. Chronic generalized eczema can be a terrible problem, and to relieve it is perhaps the greatest test of medical ability.

The approach has to be fundamental, and it seems necessary to go back to the time when eczema probably did not exist. To my mind, on the treatment of eczema hang all the law and the prophets, for eczema seems to be closely allied to all allergic manifestations. It might be the better part of wisdom if our research men temporarily abandoned their interest in hay fever and asthma and concentrated on eczema. Probably skin diseases were unknown when man lived mostly by hunting. Then the basic food was meat. The only beverage was water. Life back there was short and filled with natural and supernatural terrors, but it had its good side. Every weakling was bred out. Something we should never forget is that the ability to live successfully on that simple routine is the common inheritance of mankind.

Some years ago a determined-looking little woman came in to see me with her eight-year-old son in tow.

The opening gun was: "I want my Harry fixed so he will stay fixed."

I took a look at Harry and my soul was filled with resentment. He was covered with a thick weeping crust from top to bottom and kept scratching away at his eyelids. The skin lesion had persisted since infancy and a stench of rancid oil filled the room. "Look," I said, "I am sorry for your trouble but I am neither a pediatrician nor a skin man. Those fellows know too much about their specialties for me to compete with them."

She snapped back with, "I've tried them all. Last month my bill at the drugstore was forty-two dollars. They say you have different ideas. I have nothing to lose."

When a redheaded woman gets the bit in her teeth you might as well relax, so I sighed and said, "Let me hear the story."

Harry had suffered with eczema since birth. A maternal grandfather had died of a ruptured duodenal ulcer and a paternal grandmother had headaches and some sort of skin trouble most of her life. Harry had apparently caught it from both sides of the family. Recently cortisone had given some relief and then seemed to lose its effect. His teeth were bad.

The dentist was complaining bitterly and said that more calcium in the food was needed. Nine cavities in Harry's teeth had been filled at the last session, and now he had many more.

Physical examination revealed nothing other than the generalized weeping eczema, a heavily coated tongue, and the aforementioned bad teeth. Another session with the dentist was in order. The mother was told that "new" foods like milk and cream and cheese and ice cream and chocolate and eggs and wheat were taboo. Harry was desensitized (if that is what it is—no one knows for sure) with milk peptone. The skin lesion began to clear with the third injection. Harry was told to report ten days after the ninth injection but failed to show up.

Three years went by. The secretary came in to tell me that a woman wanted to see me on a personal matter. It proved to be Harry's mother, filled with a story that she thought I ought to know about. When Harry's eczema had completely cleared up she had forgotten about it. She was mainly interested in his teeth. It seems that a dental survey had been made of the school that Harry attended. And there at Wednesday morning auditorium the chief of the dental service had given an address in which he stated that there was only one boy in the school free from unfilled cavities in the teeth. Then Harry was called up on the platform and congratulated. "Now, Harry," said the chief dentist, "I want you to tell the boys how many glasses of milk you drink each day."

And Harry blurted out, "My doctor won't let me touch the darned stuff."

Chapter XIII

"I FEEL SICK ALL OVER"

THE LACK of interest in allergy on the part of some of the medical profession, and the strong desire on the part of people to find some miraculous drug that will cure their afflictions, leads to patients being what is called "kicked around."

Let's take an ordinary case in point. Not quite ordinary perhaps because the particular patient I have in mind had spent twenty-five years and a great deal of money in investigations.

A couple of years ago a Mrs. Evans came into the office to deposit six sets of X rays from different well-known clinics on my desk. Then there was another big envelope filled with sheaves of reports. She looked at me hopelessly and said, "I've been to twenty different physicians in this country and abroad and been surveyed twice in three big clinics and I still feel sick all over." The woman was a lady, valiantly trying to keep her emotions under control. That arouses any physician's sympathy, and you ask her for the story.

She only knew two of her grandparents but she distinctly remembered that "Granny" had sick headaches all her life. Her father was operated upon twice without relief for a dreadful pain in his face called tic douloureux. He died of blood poisoning following a drainage operation for phlebitis. Her mother vacationed in the mountains all summer long to avoid hay fever, and was ill throughout all of her pregnancies. One brother died at nineteen of tuberculosis. One sister couldn't wear an evening dress because of pustular acne on her back.

All of it was a straightaway family history of allergy on both sides of the family. The phlebitis which killed her father could have been secondary to neglected athlete's foot, that being the common cause.

As to her personal history, she had been a delicate baby and inclined to vomit all her food. She had had pneumonia in childhood and twice since. At the age of twelve she was drained for six weeks for a ruptured appendix. Many investigations had been made as to whether the stump of the appendix had been left in at the time of operation but there was no evidence that it had. Her periods had always given excruciating pain until childbirth. They were still regular. During two pregnancies her ankles had swollen to tremendous size. She had never been able to get enough sleep and was constantly exhausted. She felt dopey when she woke up in the morning and it was two hours before she felt alert. This condition is known as allergic stupor. Whenever she went out on a boat or in bright sunshine shingles developed on her lips.

The present trouble was the sense of utter exhaustion and splitting headaches. She had been belching gas and suffering with colicky abdominal pain since the age of twenty-one. She had constant lower back pain. Variously she had been treated for duodenal ulcer, a low blood pressure, a low blood sugar, a calcium deficiency, a vitamin deficiency, a herniated disc (for which she had refused operation), a fallen stomach, low thyroid, a streptococcus infection, anemia, and a high cholesterol. If I thought she was a neurasthenic she was going to quit right now. She was fed up with sedation and tranquilizers. She had run the full gamut of what is called "sucker diagnosis" in medicine. Mind you, physicians believe these things when they accuse patients of having them. It is just that the doctors haven't had enough experience at the autopsy table.

Examinations of the X rays she brought in showed nothing of importance but an irritable duodenum with no retention in the stomach, and a marked spinal curvature that can go with musical talent or some other type of sensitive nervous system.

On physical examination instant trouble was encountered. A heavily coated tongue was associated with a particularly foul breath. She had forgotten to tell me about the breath. That was the worst thing of all. For many years her husband had insisted on a separate bedroom because of it.

She had the puffs under the eyes that are probably due to chronic hives, and not alcholic dissipation. I was able to express some blackheads from her back. These had annoyed her for years. She could bend her back without bending her knees. That ruled out any serious spinal disease. Fluoroscopy was interesting. She had the tiny heart that does with a long-lived individual, and a totally opacified right antrum. There was no nasal discharge so there was no indication to drain what had apparently been an old abscess in the antrum. Nature had healed it in. But sinus trouble is a brand on you, just like a brand on a steer down in Texas. Only the allergics have sinus trouble. That was enough to clinch the diagnosis of allergy, and yet in twenty-five years, and in examination and treatment by many physicians, not one single solitary soul had ever mentioned the word. Such things are a bit discouraging. After all, allergy has been somewhat in the forefront in medicine for thirty years. But it takes lots of time to change medical thinking.

The patient was told that she could expect to feel somewhat improved in seventy-two hours. A bad breath is one of the hardest things in medicine to clear up. It might take some time—perhaps three months—but the bad breath was the thing to watch. The liver had been insulted for many years with foods which it had no power to digest. Some time would have to pass before her liver could be expected to trust her not to embarrass it. When the time came she could expect that most of the other symptoms would clear with the coated tongue and heavy breath.

Then I dictated a letter that she could study.

"Dear Mrs. Evans:

"You inherit five forms of allergy: Vulnerable skin as shown by the blackheads. Vulnerable mucous membrane as shown by the sinus trouble which nature has apparently healed in, the coated tongue and bad breath, the irritable stomach (never have complete confidence in the diagnosis of duodenal ulcer until you vomit blood or see tarry stools, neither of which you have had), and the history of ruptured appendix. Vulnerable blood vessels as shown by the puffs under the eyes (a probable form of hives), the migraine, the history of painful periods, the sense of exhaustion (a probable form of internal hives), the allergic stupor. (The liver only screens the blood for about eight hours. Then the tide probably reverses. If you stay in bed longer than eight hours you can expect to go into a poisonous stupor.)

"Physical allergy as shown by your tendency to shingles when exposed to short rays of light.

"Bacterial and virus allergy as shown by the pneumonia susceptibility.

"With all this you are still a long-lived type with a small heart. Your principal danger is of dying in another attack of pneumonia. Vaccinating every three years with the peptone in freshly boiled skimmed milk seems to protect against pneumonia for three years. That will be started today. You will have nine injections at the rate of three times a week. Put a card in the mirror of your bureau with the date when it is to be repeated, May 27, 1960. You remember the date.

"Your routine is as follows:

"In bed at 11 P.M. after setting the alarm clock for 7 A.M.

"7 A.M. out of bed.

"Swing your back thirty times on arising and again before lunch and before dinner. Be careful to do it correctly. Probably if you were killed in an automobile smashup and immediately autopsied, because your physician wanted to know why you complained so bitterly about backache, the only finding would be blood vessels that seemed too small for the job of holding you upright. Apparently what is needed is to grow new blood vessels or to increase the size of the old ones. That is accomplished by gentle rhythmic back swinging, starting slowly. As that is persisted in you will find that you will become able to put the palms of your hands flat on the floor after the tenth swing. Most people like you are free from backache after they have persisted in the exercise for ninety days. I will show you how it is performed.

"7:20 A.M. leave the house to walk outdoors for thirty

minutes. After you have walked ten minutes you can expect bile to begin to drain from your liver and gall bladder into the bowel. In the last twenty minutes of the thirty-minute walk you can expect to drain a pint of bile. This carries off a tremendous lot of overnight waste from the body. Of all the things you are told to do in the management of allergy, this thirty-minute walk is the most important. If it is raining in the morning go later in the day, even though it is not as good. Get some walking shoes, and carry a police whistle around your neck in plain sight. In the wintertime wear a ski suit, and it might be a good idea to get a nylon rain suit with a hood so you can walk in light rain.

"As to food, remember this. There is one particularly happy combination of food that seems to work so well in all the sixty or so common manifestations of allergy that it is called 'the allergic bandwagon.' It doesn't matter too much whether duodenal ulcer or tic douloureux or hives or asthma or chronic sinus trouble is being treated, three meals a day of steak or chops without salt, boiled or baked potatoes without butter, and canned pears seem the best. I want you to stick rigidly on that until the injections are finished. Then an effort will be made to expand your food. Two double rib Frenched chops with the backbone cut off and one rib cut completely out of the bottom seem to agree the best and taste the best. If your bowels are not moving well switch to sirloin steak with some hard gristle and outside fat. If enough gristle is eaten no trouble with constipation need be expected.

"Potatoes in the morning can be sliced thin and boiled seventeen minutes, or else they can be boiled ten minutes, the water poured off, and then fried in beef dripping or corn oil. Home-canned fruit is almost always better than anything you can buy, so if you know anyone who has some good home-canned pears try to get them. Water is the most important single food and you must be meticulous about drinking it. The best way is to put your quota for the day, six glasses, in a thermos pitcher in the living room. Starting in half an hour after breakfast, finish three glasses one half hour before lunch. Then start in again one half hour after lunch to finish three glasses one half hour before dinner.

"The only medicine of any kind that you are allowed is hot water. The tap water can be shifted to that if distress in the stomach persists."

The woman did exceedingly well. Her tongue began to clear on the third day and the breath was normal by the end of the second month. The backache vanished.

The thing that interested me most was that when the time came to expand her food she developed into a splendid cook. She learned to make excellent sauces, using potato flour, pie filling that was out of this world, and mouth-watering stews of fat meat. Her husband was as pleased as she was. A few weeks ago she came into the office quite disturbed. The family were moving out West, and what would she do about repeating her injections when they came due? So I gave her the following directions to give to her physician out there:

Fill a large (75-cc.) test tube (Pyrex) two thirds full of ordinary skimmed fresh milk. Cover the test tube of milk with an inverted 30-cc. beaker and place in a large (1-liter) beaker filled with water. Boil the whole thing on an asbestos mat over an ordinary gas flame or electric stove or bunsen burner for twenty minutes. This material keeps all day long at room temperature if kept covered with the small beaker and flamed every time it is used.

From this test tube, the milk is sucked up in a freshly boiled small Luer syringe. The skin should be prepared with tincture of iodine. The site of the injection should vary—

right deltoid, left deltoid, right thigh, left thigh. If the injection is put in an area which is still red from a previous injection, an Arthus' phenomenon (circular slough) may take place, so be careful to alternate the areas. The injections are given as follows:

1st dose—¼ cc. (⅛ cc. in the skin and ⅛ cc. underneath)

2nd dose—½ cc. (⅛ cc. in the skin and ⅜ cc. underneath)

3rd dose—¾ cc. (⅛ cc. in the skin and ⅝ cc. underneath)

4th dose—1 cc. (⅛ cc. in the skin and ⅞ cc. underneath)

5th dose—1¼ cc. (⅛ cc. in the skin and 1⅛ cc. underneath)

6th dose—1½ cc. (⅛ cc. in the skin and 1⅜ cc. underneath)

7th dose—1¾ cc. (⅛ cc. in the skin and 1⅝ cc. underneath)

8th dose—2 cc. (⅛ cc. in the skin and 1⅞ cc. underneath)

9th dose—2 cc. (⅛ cc. in the skin and 1⅞ cc. underneath)

Supposedly different systems in the body are stimulated when the skin is irritated as well as the tissues under the skin.

Adrenalin should always be handy for any general reactions, such as asthma attacks or hives, though I have never seen a general reaction when only nine injections in all have been given. The general reactions I have seen have come after using eighteen injections when it was customary to give twenty-four in all. As a rule, it is rather encouraging to see some local red reactions (blushing) after the injections. If the reactions are severe, the dosage can be kept the same or de-

creased. The chance of improvement of allergic manifestations seems to be about eight out of ten. Injections should
probably be repeated every three years. They seem to modify
greatly or eliminate many allergic disorders for that length of
time. Particularly do they seem to modify migraine and prevent lobar pneumonia and reduce common colds to two a
year. Injections are customarily given three times a week. Try
not to allow more than seven days to elapse between injections. I haven't seen it, but it seems possible to have a severe
reaction if the interval between injections is longer than that.

I received a fine long letter from Mrs. Evans at Christmas-
time. She said that she was feeling completely well and had
been sticking to her routine like glue.

She had better continue to stick like glue, for allergy isn't
something you cure. The routine is a way of life by which
trouble is avoided.

Many disease processes that afflict us are supposedly in-
duced by a kind of protein called peptone. Supposedly it is
the peptone contained in a pneumonia germ that makes us
sick when we contract pneumonia. It is the peptone in a
tuberculosis germ that dissolves the lung and causes cavity
formation. Peptone in house dust can give rise to bronchial
asthma in some people. And peptone in the creamed chicken
and ice cream served at a children's party can give rise to the
peptone shock which may induce croup in some of the susceptible children.

Probably vaccination against particular infectious organ-
isms such as those causing typhoid fever is not nearly as
specific as it was hoped it would be. Resistance to the particular peptone in the typhoid bacillus can possibly be raised
by vaccination with some other kind of peptone. Much good
research work is needed on this problem. At present there is
no certainty that it is lack of resistance to irritation from

peptone that is responsible for so much human misery. When protein material is derived from outside of the human body it is called foreign protein. Probably it is owing to the peptone content in this foreign protein that injection of increasing amounts tends to build up resistance to offending substances floating in the blood stream. But no one knows for sure. Various foreign proteins have been tried out to see which seems to produce the most resistance with the least unpleasant reaction. In my hands Witte's peptone spleen liquid and typhoid and other bacterial vaccines have proven uncontrollable. Some of the reactions patients have experienced have been unpleasant to say the least.

But vaccination with the peptone in freshly boiled milk, if that is what the body defenses are being raised against, does seem to raise resistance to many irritants, and in the office something like 270,000 individual injections have been given to patients, without any general reactions seen.

The words "peptone" and "foreign protein" are used interchangeably in this writing. The important thing is to use a kind of peptone which promotes maximal resistance to peptone irritants and yet has no harmful side effects. In my experience the peptone in freshly boiled skimmed milk seems to answer these requirements.

Chapter XIV

BACTERIAL AND VIRUS ALLERGY

WHEN IT COMES to fighting infection not everything in the practice of medicine is sweetness and light. Wonderful strides have been made of course. Typhoid fever and smallpox and mastoiditis are rarely encountered any more. A good deal of hookworm, malaria, tuberculosis, rheumatic fever, and syphilis is fairly well controlled. We don't expect to encounter plague or yellow fever at all. Many erstwhile problems have yielded to improved sanitation and better food, the wearing of better shoes, mosquito control, national immunity, vaccination, and in some few cases to potent new drugs. Still and all the amount of time lost in industry from illness is a matter of concern. Sickness can appreciably increase the cost of production in a factory, and it can strain the family budget to the limit.

The common cold is the main villain in this respect. Usually it is of viral origin accompanied by a secondary infection with bacteria. A virus is a living infectious agent causing disease. Usually a virus is small enough to pass through a porous stone filter and too small to be seen by an ordinary micro-scope.

If anything, common colds seem to be increasingly preva-lent. Many reasons have been advanced for this but there is no scientific proof of any one cause.

The common cold is not a reportable disease so the exact incidence is in doubt.

Two or three generations ago only the strongest children survived. Now thanks to the skill of our obstetricians many of the more delicate women can produce living babies. Then clever pediatricians take over and bring the children up to maturity. All of which makes for a less disease-resistant race. The biologists are a ruthless bunch, and quite devoid of any particular regard for doctors. In theory they don't even want a surgeon to patch up a man who has been hit on the head with a brick, the argument being that it is better for the human race to be able to dodge bricks. Which is a correct viewpoint, I suppose, unless it happens to be your head and your brick.

The contagious nature of the common cold is obvious to anyone, but has been particularly well demonstrated by using the ferret as an experimental animal. This member of the weasel family contracts a viral cold with great ease. An ab-solutely windless tunnel twenty feet long, two feet in diame-ter, and bent at right angles can be constructed. At one end of the tunnel is placed a cage containing a ferret that has been inoculated with a viral cold. At the other end a healthy ferret is placed in another cage. Within a few hours the healthy ferret contracts the cold. It is small wonder that these pan-demics of influenza sweep over the world.

The crowded conditions in which many of us work and live promote the spread of infection. Factories, big staffs in offices, the subways, theaters, stores, the military services—all can be blamed.

In the wintertime steam heat is an undoubted factor. The air gets too dry to suit the nasal mucous membranes and opens the gates to infection. Almost a hogshead of water a day is needed to moisten the air of an ordinary room properly when steam heat is on full. I know a physicist who is cursed with head colds. The treatment employed horrifies his wife. He goes around with a watering can and saturates all the rugs. But even that doesn't approach a hogshead full of water, while a steaming teakettle is just a joke.

Air conditioning may play some part. If you have ever lived in France you have undoubtedly found people completely sold on the idea that any draft of air is dangerous. Local chilling could be responsible for lowered resistance. It is a debatable point. In the North many people blame their head colds on the air conditioning. However, in the deep South office efficiency seems markedly increased by the use of it.

Food and drink are apparently of tremendous importance in increased or lowered resistance to common colds. But before discussing them it might be well to consider the two main types with which we have to deal, the contagious and the non-contagious cold. The latter opens the way to a lot of bunk. Many of us, when we get too tired or are exposed to too much light, muscular exertion, anxiety, alcohol, bad food, or constipation, can wake up with a raspy throat. There is no fever, but aching pains throughout the body, prostration, and a wet nose all suggest that we are coming down with a cold. A good bowel movement gained with something like epsom salts and a night's sleep result in a feeling of well-being and the conviction that we have "thrown the cold off." No one catches this kind of a cold from anyone else. You can credit almost anything you please for the good result—a Dover's powder, or two stiff drinks, a hot bath, massage, sniffing ammonia, a nasal spray, a dose of penicillin. Apparently all of the symptoms were due to some unknown irritant, other than a virus, floating in the blood stream. The liver took over and a good bowel movement and good night's sleep were followed by cure.

But the common contagious cold grinds along remorselessly through all of its various stages and continues to defy any specific treatment. Efforts to prevent it by viral vaccination have not been impressive so far. Treatment with the powerful new antibiotics and sulfa drugs seems useless and can prolong the prostration by adding the shattering effect of drug therapy to the load. Then too antibiotics and sulfa drugs may induce an attack of hives which is worse than the cold.

The feeling that something heroic must be done right now about a contagious cold has resulted in the promiscuous use of the new wonder drugs. Millions of people have had useless jabs of penicillin for ordinary head colds, in consequence of which hundreds of viruses and all sorts of bacteria have taken on increased resistance, just as houseflies do when subjected to some new spray. Wonder drugs should usually be reserved for fevers of one hundred and two degrees or over, and where a real threat of pneumonia exists.

Every physician has his own pet way of alleviating—I said "alleviating," not "curing"—a bad cold. Mine happens to be a couple of heaping teaspoons of epsom salts in a half glass of ice water as a starter. Twelve hours after taking this there can be the odor of hydrogen sulphide gas, the same thing noted on a clam flat at low tide, in the bowel movement. When this is present, for some unknown reason, the head feels clearer. Then I tell the patient that the liver has two important functions. One is to screen the blood of irritants, including virus and bacterial infections. A contagious cold is a blood-stream infection with virus. Another function of the liver is to make sugar. Conceivably a liver that is given lots of sugar can devote more time to killing bugs. Farfetched perhaps, but at least it has more logic to it than anything else I know of in the treatment of contagious colds. I ask the patient to buy eighteen lemons and a box of brown sugar. Every day for three days a pitcher of lemonade is consumed within one three-hour period. A pitcherful consists of the juice of six lemons, six tablespoons of brown or white sugar, six glasses of water, and some ice. A glass of this is drunk every thirty minutes for six doses on three succeeding days. Meals need not be missed. Aspirin is used to allay aching pain, and only triple bromide used to allay cough. It seems as good a treatment as any.

One thing that always has to be kept in mind is that maybe a head cold is a good thing and that nature doesn't want us to develop a specific treatment for it. A bad cold could be a fine way to raise resistance to the hordes of infections with which we must do battle in order to survive.

Some things seem peculiarly undesirable in the treatment of a contagious cold. In "the good old days" it was customary for a businessman with a contagious cold to stop in the doctor's office on his way downtown. A strong nasal spray with plenty of cocaine would "open his nose." Inspired by the cocaine, he would feel better temporarily and go down to the office to infect everyone in sight. Such a procedure is not highly regarded nowadays, for we know the nasal mucous membrane can be easily injured.

An emulsion of a child's spinal cord obtained immediately after a death from poliomyelitis can be sprayed into the nose of a susceptible monkey. The monkey will not contract polio. But if, preceding this performance, the monkey's nose has been sprayed with argyrol, silver nitrate, cocaine, or even plain mineral oil, then infection with polio can take place like a shot. No! The nose is holy ground. Whenever possible, stay out of it.

The reason for listing marked susceptibility to contagious colds as an allergic manifestation is the response to anti-allergic treatment which many of us seem to show. Marked susceptibility may be shown by the contraction of more than two contagious colds a year. Only two a year seems a reasonable number about which we should have no legitimate complaint. But when it comes to six or eight a year a definite lack of resistance seems to be present. The family and personal history may be loaded with allergic manifestations but that is a doubtful factor. Only when the pattern is well established and the colds sharply reduced in number does preventive treatment mean anything. Forty years of experience with allergic patients has convinced me that in such people contagious colds can be markedly reduced by adherence to primitive food and by vaccination with foreign protein. What part the routine nine injections of foreign protein every three years plays I don't know, I only know that it seems to work. A good guess would be that it represents one third of the importance in any anti-allergic routine. Probably it is particularly important in the prevention of lobar pneumonia. Allergic people seem prone to develop pneumonia. Some of my patients have had as many as seven attacks before falling into my hands. For three years after vaccination with foreign protein they seem to remain free of attacks of lobar pneumonia. About seventy of these patients, with a history of previous attacks of pneumonia, have failed to repeat their injections at the end of three years. Sometime in the next two years another attack of pneumonia has developed in each of these seventy people. That was sufficient to make firm believers of them, and now they are meticulous in repeating injections every thirty-six months. Such evidence is merely suggestive, but it may be possible to prevent a lot of pneumonia.

The rough impression I have gained over the years is that one quarter of the patients subjected to the series of injections and restricted to primitive food have no contagious colds whatever for three years. Sixty-five per cent seem to be reduced to the normal number of two contagious colds a year, and ten per cent seem to derive no benefit.

Such figures can mean next to nothing at all. Office practice does not lend itself to scientific work. Still the impression is there and the group that have been susceptible to contagious colds, and then become entirely free for three years, are particularly gratified.

One thing that should never be forgotten in any evaluation of preventive treatment is the effect of age. Some people, who have been susceptible to frequent contagious colds all of their lives, may suddenly take on increased resistance around the age of sixty. From then on, and without treatment of any kind, they may become free from attacks.

And that is just one of the difficulties in evaluating the treatment of common colds.

Poliomyelitis is much in the public eye at present. It is a virus infection which invades the body through the nasal mucous membrane, or more commonly perhaps through the mucous membrane lining the gastrointestinal tract. Then the nervous system can be sharply involved. The disease is comparatively rare and the ordinary practicing physician may encounter only one or two cases in his medical lifetime. But the tragic consequences that can follow invasion of the spinal cord in the paralytic form focuses a good deal of attention on it.

The diagnosis of infection with poliomyelitis virus can be

incorrect. Coxsackie virus, Echo virus, mumps virus, herpes simplex virus, and St. Louis encephalitis virus can all imitate to some extent invasion by the poliomyelitis virus. But fortunately any weakness or paralysis that may develop in these other conditions is likely to be transient and is less likely to have a fatal outcome. The reasons for listing poliomyelitis as a possible manifestation of allergy are mostly in the family and previous or subsequent personal history of the children who survive an attack. In my exceedingly limited experience they all seem to have a positive history. So far all of the children I have seen have been milk drinkers and it is known now that infection can take place through the digestive tract. Up to date I know of no child with eczema, who is under anti-allergic treatment with restriction of the "big bad seven" in food, and vaccination to build up resistance to peptone irritation every three years, who has contracted polio. Which again, because of the limited number of children, could mean next to nothing.

However, the fact worries me enough to put these restrictions on children when polio is prevalent in the town in which they live.

1. If the parents have money enough to afford it, they should get out of town. A pack train trip in the mountains for six weeks will probably free the children from exposure.

2. Avoid swimming pools as you would the Devil. Running water has a tendency to clean itself of infection in something like eight miles, but a swimming pool is a lot different than running water. The virus may be already in the nose and all set to invade as soon as the nasal mucous membrane is injured by water. Keep your head above any water when there is polio around.

3. No milk or cheese or ice cream or chocolate or eggs or wheat are to be delivered to the house. There are plenty of

other things to eat, and it may be the peptone or something
else in those foods that lowers resistance. The infection itself
actually could be milk-borne.

4. No one knows as yet exactly how good polio vaccine is,
but it seems reasonable to think that it might offer a little
worth-while protection up to the age of seventeen.

The conservative attitude of some physicians concerning
polio vaccine needs explanation. It is realized, of course, that
emotional people regard polio vaccine as some sort of manna
from heaven. Anyone who casts doubt on its efficacy is viewed
as a heretic.

But what physicians are interested in is the truth and so
far, after some years of intensive use of the vaccine, there
seems to be no definite decrease in the disease. We know
that viral vaccines for influenza and contagious colds have not
been particularly efficient. Many of us have seen dreadful reactions, with permanent injury to the nervous system, from
such simple things as smallpox vaccination. There are four
problems to be considered in any mass immunization of a
nation.

1. Is the disease becoming less severe and less prevalent because of gradually acquired nationwide immunity? That is the
situation in tuberculosis today. To judge this in polio requires close observation of a group of 500,000 children for
about fifteen years with no treatment whatever.

2. Does the particular vaccine in question reduce the expected morbidity rate in a closely observed group of 500,000
children?

3. Is a different vaccine—ordinary typhoid vaccine, for instance, or foreign protein like freshly boiled skimmed milk—
just as efficient in increasing resistance as the supposedly specific polio vaccine? Five hundred thousand children are
needed as a control group. Any vaccine with peptone in it

might increase resistance to polio. A comparison is needed.

4. Does food make a difference? It would be a fearful job to get 500,000 children to do without milk and the other six foods that seem bad in allergy but it might be important. If we had such evidence as that, fifteen years from now we might know something about polio. But unfortunately the program went off half cocked, and now it seems that we will be debating for years the importance or unimportance of the vaccine.

One thing that is definitely bad about the effort is the propaganda against tonsillectomy for children in the summertime. The summertime is the ideal time to do a tonsillectomy because of the lowered incidence of respiratory infections. You would practically need a microscope to find the rate of paralytic polio among children who have had their tonsils out in the summertime. Still the propaganda is there and the much-sought-after operating rooms lie practically idle during June, July, and August. Tonsillectomy at the proper time can be of great importance in keeping a child healthy.

With any infection that is under study it is desirable to keep an open mind. Perhaps the newest idea in medicine is that markedly allergic people are unwise in visiting or continuing to live in areas where malaria is prevalent. It has been my experience to observe some obvious allergics who seemed unusually susceptible to malaria. Soldiers, convalescing from heavy malarial infections, can be kept in a hospital for two months during which time they are free from fever. Then they are given a pass and go downtown to have some drinks. Back they come with a temperature of one hundred and six degrees. There could be an allergic factor in it. Never expect to enjoy alcohol without ill effects if you have allergy.

As to milk, one hesitates to cast suspicion on a great industry from which many millions of people derive a living, but I can't help worrying about little things that have been observed.

Hospital internes are notably susceptible to glandular fever, and hospital internes are notable milk drinkers.

A milk handler in a dairy supplying most of a small city can contract yellow jaundice (infectious hepatitis). Within a two-month period seven hundred people in the city can and do develop infectious hepatitis.

It is something to worry about.

Chapter XV

VULNERABLE MUCOUS MEMBRANE

SHOCK TISSUE, the ability of certain cells to fiercely resent irritants when it involves mucous membrane, can take many forms, all of them more or less unpleasant.

If an irritant which the liver seems unable to handle floats in the blood stream, a sebaceous gland in an eyelid can be inflamed. A probable secondary infection with staphyolcoccus can result in abscess formation. This may resolve itself, or it may require incision and drainage. Adjacent sebaceous glands can become involved and a whole series of styes develop. Some people will develop a sty within six hours after eating chocolate or strawberries. The intake of any one of the "big bad seven"—milk, cream, cheese, ice cream, chocolate, eggs, wheat flour—as well as alcohol can result in sty formation. Many patients rapidly learn which of the minor irritants (orange juice for instance) induces their trouble.

Treatment involves avoidance of the cause and then vaccination. Bacterial vaccines, with the possible exception of typhoid vaccine, can all be somewhat uncontrollable. Violent reactions can occur. It seems probable that it is the peptone in the vaccine that does the most good. The safest and the most efficient vaccination in my hands has been the ordinary foreign protein in freshly boiled skimmed milk.

A constantly wet nose and the scraping of secretions in the back of the throat called postnasal drip both stem from blood irritation. In order to add the moisture necessary for oxygen interchange in the lungs to air that is breathed in, the nose needs to be reasonably well obstructed by turbinates—folds of membrane that give off moisture to the air going to the lungs. A big hole in each nostril is undesirable. To supply the extra moisture to incoming air the nose needs a monstrous blood supply, so that the first place blood irritants running wild may be manifest is in the nose. Sneezing and snoring can be evidence of that. Many people will snore their heads off after having eaten ice cream for dessert.

Sinus trouble used to be a rough experience. Now we know that the inflamed sinuses that occasionally require surgical intervention are the antra in the upper cheekbones. These hollow spaces, about the size of an acorn, are lined with mucous membrane and seem to function as sounding boards for the voice. Other sinuses, the sphenoids and ethmoids and the mastoids and frontals, are usually best treated conservatively without surgery or else with the potent new drugs. Indeed it is beginning to be difficult to demonstrate to a resident interne in a big specialty hospital the correct technique of operation on the mastoid. A year may go by before a suitable case is admitted. But I have seen a neglected case, which might have been saved by good surgery, die of meningitis secondary to pus formation in an ethmoid sinus. Such things are unusual.

As to an infected antrum, the attitude toward that has changed. Time was when such a condition seemed to require treatment by irrigation for months or years. Nowadays the attending physician should usually spot the condition. A head cold that hangs on and a foggy voice suggest acute infection of an antrum. Fluoroscopic examination or X-ray films confirm the diagnosis. In the absence of complications such as high fever or nasal hemorrhage, or dimness of vision in the eye above the antrum, or joint pain, the physician may delay reference of the patient to a competent nose and throat man until twenty-one days from the apparent time of onset. This allows Nature to get in her healing effect. The patient meanwhile is kept on the allergic bandwagon of fat meat and potatoes and canned pears and is vaccinated with foreign protein. About nine out of ten patients can have infected antra resolved by these methods. The one who does not is promptly turned over to the nose and throat man.

His methods also have changed greatly. In the old days a rattail filelike instrument would be crashed through the wall of the antrum and brutally dragged back and forth. The scar tissue resultant upon this attack would promptly close over the hole and drainage would stop. Nowadays the antrum is gently irrigated through the natural opening from the nose. The color of the washed-out material may be bright yellow or bright green, or gray mucous can come out with a plop like a dead oyster. Putrefaction may have set in and the odor of the washed-out material can be horrible. Washings continue, and usually only three or four are needed, until the return is clear or until X ray shows that the antrum is not opacified. If, in spite of regular washing, the infection continues, it may be necessary to admit the patient to a hospital. There, under general anesthesia, and after a fracture dislocation of a turbinate, a window the size of a dime is made in the bottom of the antrum. This results in permanent and usually perfect drainage and the trouble can be expected to be over for all time.

One of the new and good things in medicine is the routine inspection in the course of physical examination of the antra by the fluoroscope. Considerable objection on the part of X-ray men who like to study films has had to be met. No permanent record is available of course. The method requires some experience, but apparently it should be a routine part of every physical examination. I understand that recently one of the big nose and throat clinics in London began using fluoroscopy of the antra as a routine procedure. For myself, and after twenty-five years of experience with the method, I think it is most helpful in diagnosis. To some extent I have rather pioneered the procedure and wish it was more generally employed. All that is needed after examining the chest is to tilt the head well back. Then the fluoroscope is raised and the antra inspected.

Reflex cough is common when an antrum is blocked and in the past many patients have had unnecessary treatment for pulmonary tuberculosis when the whole trouble lay in an antrum. I have yet to see a patient with antritis who failed to show in the family and personal history and physical examination other evidence of allergy, so that I think it is proof of the condition.

Drugs seem to have little if any value in the treatment of antritis. After X-ray examination has spotted the trouble, there seems to be no way to predict what the nose and throat man will find when he has to wash out an antrum. Pre-existing infection may have been walled in by dense scar tissue and nothing may be obtained on washing. Such a condition is somewhat out of the ordinary. More commonly old abscesses continue to slowly drain over the mucous membrane of the nose. This irritation is followed by polyp formation. Nasal polypi when noted should always require a search for the underlying sinusitis.

The patient who has had an attack of antritis (sinus trouble) seems to have opened a door to subsequent infection, so that two forms of activity are permanently restricted. Don't blow your nose. Wipe it. Blowing blasts on a handkerchief with a head cold can blow infection sideways into the antra. Then too remember that an animal that lives in air and water, like the hippopotamus, has a valve to shut off the nose while submerged. That valve protects the delicate nasal mucous membrane from injury by water. Humans have no such protective mechanism. Diving and the overhand stroke are not wise if you have ever had sinus trouble. Just lower yourself off the dock into the water and use a breast stroke.

Apparently it isn't a matter of dirty water. Any water can bother nasal mucous membrane. The incidence of sinus trouble is supposed to be just about as high when diving into crystal-clear Florida springs delivering eight thousand gallons of water a minute as it is in Gowanus Canal in Brooklyn.

A coated tongue and heavy brassy breath both seem to be evidence of a liver that is not scavenging the blood properly. Many things that we eat and drink enter the blood stream more or less unchanged. The liver has the job of seeing that they are broken down into harmless substances and that the waste products are eliminated. When it fails in this function the tongue and the breath can undergo all sorts of changes, including that suggesting the classic description of "the floor of a chicken house." Treatment is directed toward avoiding bad food and drink, taking hard daily outdoor exercise, and vaccination with foreign protein which in some unknown way seems to stimulate the liver. A cathartic or enema habit just seems to make the condition worse. Along with proper food and water intake the patient has to be trained into normal bowel function. Acute and chronic infections can coat a tongue as long as they last but that is a different matter. The ordinary coated tongue and heavy brassy breath should be thought of as evidence of shock tissue.

A large majority of disorders involving the stomach and small and large bowel seem to have a big allergic element.

An ordinary meal taken by a healthy person is churned in the stomach into a condition like whipped cream. While this is going on, the pylorus, the distal end of the stomach, remains closed by strong muscles. The churning effect is accomplished by about eight hundred muscular waves which pass over the walls during stomach digestion. At the proper time the muscles in the pylorus relax and allow food to pass into the small intestine. When this rhythm is interfered with for one reason or another, all sorts of things can happen. Loss of appetite, belching of gas, regurgitation of sour material into the esophagus, a feeling of distress, nausea, vomiting, mild, moderate, severe, or terrible pain, are all linked under the word "pylorospasm." It is a poor descriptive term, implying as it does that a cramp in the end of the stomach is responsible for the misery. But for want of something better, the word is still in use to describe any or all of the symptoms mentioned.

The best explanation of abdominal unhappiness seems to come from studies of the contraction waves in the stomach walls of patients who have swallowed collapsed balloons. The balloons are inflated and the contraction waves recorded on revolving smoked drums. Healthy normal people after a regular meal may have eight hundred regular strong waves. But in the presence of pylorospasm these waves may be irregular, too weak or too strong, and increase in number to four thousand. We haven't been able to derive much help from the studies of gastric chemistry. The answer seems to be in correcting the mechanical disorder.

Walter Hamburger in Chicago did much of the pioneering work on pylorospasm. His figures for the various causes of increased gastric contractions ran roughly as follows:

20% had cancer or ulcer of the stomach
20% had duodenal ulcer or gallstones
20% had appendicitis or kidney stones or lesions elsewhere in the abdomen
20% had active syphilis or tuberculosis
20% were nervous

Such an interpretation would not be accepted nowadays. The years have convinced me that nothing lies like a series of X rays, especially where it concerns the diagnosis of duodenal ulcer. Time was when it would seem that ninety per cent of the diagnoses of duodenal ulcer were wrong. Nowadays ordinary X-ray laboratories may only make errors to the extent of sixty per cent. What they should report is that the duodenum (the first part of the small intestine) is deformed and irritable from some unknown cause. What many of them do report is "ulcer." Just think that over for a moment. Spasm of the muscle in the pylorus, or adhesions, can deform the duodenum. The tiniest hole in the mucous membrane in the nose usually results in a nosebleed. The wall of a small blood vessel is eaten through and bleeding results. The mucous membrane lining the first part of the small intestine is similar in some respects to that in the nose. It is difficult to punch a hole in it without eating through the wall of a blood vessel. That is shown by the vomiting of blood or more commonly the passage of tarry stools. Bleeding from high up in the bowel gives a black color to the stool. If you haven't had either one of those conditions, it might be a good idea to stop bragging about duodenal ulcer and go to work. All that may be required is good living and that takes some brains and more ambition.

So I would say that about ninety per cent of the causes of pylorospasm should be listed under a comparatively new name, "allergic functional pylorospasm," due to bad living. The other ten per cent you can divide any way you wish, except that active syphilis and active tuberculosis are getting to be negligible components.

Medical men have great respect for those who have been in charge of the X-ray work in a big hospital for many years. If a mistake is made the operating surgeon comes charging down to the X-ray room to find out how it happened, and that makes a good X-ray man cautious in diagnosis. When the X-ray man reports a big erosion in the wall of the stomach, to my mind it is an instant call for good surgery. There is no sure way of differentiating cancer from ulcer of the stomach. Ulcer can be cured by surgery and cancer possibly can be delayed. It seems better not to fool around with medical treatment, and to go ahead.

Duodenal ulcer is a different matter. Rarely is that malignant. It is much akin to a canker sore in the mouth. When it is acute, it can exert a tremendous reflex on the pyloric sphincter in the end of the stomach, so that a seventy-two-hour retention in the stomach of most of the food that is swallowed can occur. But if there is no evidence of perforation, there is no hurry whatever. Rest, and small doses of the same chloral that used to be used to shanghai sailors, and fluid under the skin, and only hot water by mouth, can miraculously transform the patient.

Twenty years ago I ordered a man into the hospital for violent pain and a seventy-two-hour complete retention in the stomach due to duodenal ulcer. Other evidence of allergy was present. And all I did was to stop his milk drinking. So far, under repeated observations he has stopped belching gas and is completely comfortable. Experience keeps one humble.

Irritation of the duodenum can be a tricky business. While there is little proof of it, because the patients do not require surgery, apparently it is possible to have a shallow erosion of the mucous membrane, exactly like a canker sore in the mouth, eat through the wall of a blood vessel. This may promptly follow upon the ingestion of something like ice cream or chocolate. Mild or severe hemorrhage with tarry stools results. Often transfusions are necessary to cope with weakness, collapse, thirst, and anemia. Yet two weeks later, when a gastrointestinal X ray is made, it may show nothing at all out of the ordinary. So the term "allergic duodenal erosion with negative X rays" has come into use.

When a real duodenal ulcer perforates the wall and bores into the pancreas it can cause a most shocking type of pain. This calls for instant action on the part of an experienced abdominal surgeon, the danger being that a huge blood vessel in the pancreas can be eaten through and the patient bleed to death. Proper surgery, done in time, usually results in cure.

The common thing, allergic functional pylorospasm, and the real duodenal ulcers with no tendency toward perforation or repeated hemorrhage simply require good medical care. A great many surgical statistical reports note that "the patient failed to do well on prolonged medical care and came to operation." The question is, "What medical care?" In order to teach hospital internes the new method I have done this: Two patients as nearly alike as possible are chosen in the ward. Each should have a prolonged history of distress, one or more bouts of intestinal bleeding, and positive X-ray evidence of duodenal ulcer with apparently no tendency toward perforation. Such cases are common medical problems. Careful history taking shows evidence of allergy in both family and personal histories. Almost universally the internes have been taught in medical schools the old methods of treatment. Milk and eggs or eggnog are fed to the patient every two hours, and considerable alkali to neutralize acidity is administered, and sedation is employed.

The new method recognizes that most of the digestive trouble in life is due to new foods. I repeat, anything that has come up in the past eight thousand years is regarded as new. So out of the window go milk and eggs. Nothing is allowed but primitive food and such new foods as experience suggests are well tolerated. That means the allergic bandwagon: tender fat meat without salt, potato without butter, and canned pears.

One patient is treated by the old method, and the other given only three meals a day of the above-mentioned food. The only medication allowed the patient on a diet of primitive food is changing from tap water to hot water. Hot water can be most gratifying when your stomach is contracting three or four thousand times with a meal.

Then the internes watch the patients to see what happens. The usual result is to note that the patient on primitive food becomes comfortable and goes back to work five times faster than the one treated by the older methods. As soon as possible, the one on primitive food is sent out for a thirty-minute walk before breakfast. He does all his water drinking between meals. Because he has had a hemorrhage he is advised never again to take alcohol in any manner, shape, or form. When he is comfortable the food is expanded. This would seem to be a considerable advance in the treatment of duodenal trouble.

An interruption in the form of an emergency call stopped

my scribbling about the mysteries of pylorospasm. I had to return to the office when the trouble was over. My nurse informed me that the gospel of allergy was spreading. Some organization in Nassau County had staged a chicken dinner for its members. Fifty people had become desperately ill with food poison. Only one woman, who had not eaten the chicken, was spared. My nurse asked her why she had passed up the chicken. The response was, "Because I'm allergic to ptomaine." Reports like that cheer up a physician.

But to get back to vulnerable mucous membrane. The normal reaction of a bowel to insults by bad food or cathartics, or enemas, or the colon irrigation habit, can be the production of mucous. In the old days there was a good deal of physiotherapy racketeering based on how much mucous was found in the bowel when the colon was irrigated. The amount of mucous washed out would be described in detail, and a solution of aspirin left in the bowel. The aspirin would help to alleviate any joint pain.

The bowel can become inflamed with a dreadful disease called ulcerative colitis. In such cases ulcer formation destroys the muscular coat of the bowel and converts it into a replica of a garden hose that cannot contract. Diarrhea with pus and blood accompany this. Because there always seems to be a large allergic element in this miserable disease, and because cortisone temporarily relieves it, necessary surgery may be delayed too long. The only good results in this condition that I have seen have been where the involved bowel has been removed by operation. You don't want to fool around with true ulcerative colitis. It's a killer. Fortunately, however, the diagnosis is usually wrong. If an enema bag used during a barium colon X ray is held too high, the force of gravity may flatten out the normal contractions of the large bowel. Then it may seem that the muscular coat has been destroyed and a faulty diagnosis of ulcerative colitis is made.

Many patients who don't bother to empty their bowel at the proper time may have the gut irritated by prolonged contact with stool. This can result in pinpoint hemorrhages in the bowel wall, and these may be mistaken for ulcer. The correct diagnosis in the vast majority of cases of alternating constipation and diarrhea should be that of "irritable colon." The anti-allergic routine usually cures this.

It makes a good surgeon's back hair stand up when you tell him that you think appendicitis only occurs in allergic people, and that an acute attack usually follows bad food. But I think that is probably true. It is difficult indeed to keep susceptible children away from milk and ice cream and chocolate and wheat.

The diagnosis of chronic appendicitis in children is particularly hard at times. There may be a history of repeated stomach upsets sufficiently bad to warrant sending the child home from school. Any pain may be reflex in the upper abdomen and not over the appendix. The noteworthy thing is associated constipation. Appendicitis, either acute or chronic, seems to throw a body block in the bowel and constipation is the rule. X-ray and blood examination does not help in the diagnosis in the average case. Somebody has to be tough about it and say that the child's appendix should be in a bottle, otherwise it never will be safe to go to camp in the summertime. Once the appendix is out, the attacks can be expected to stop. Surgeons don't like to do what is called "prophylactic appendectomy" but, given proper indications, it is usually a wise procedure.

At times in allergy other areas of mucous membrane can

be irritated and produce floods of mucous discharge. For that reason, some girls can't touch chocolate. And catarrh in any form always suggests that it might be a good idea to go back to the jungle.

Chapter XVI

VULNERABLE SKIN

EMERGENCIES come first, so I dropped everything and hurried down to the architect's building. There I found a red-headed man stretched out on the floor of his office surrounded by anxious draughtsmen and blueprints. He was conscious and when I asked him what the trouble was he feebly pointed to the region of his heart. A hasty examination showed that his heart was not enlarged and was contracting regularly at a terrific rate, perhaps around two hundred a minute. Unaided, it is impossible to record accurately a heart rate of over one hundred and forty a minute but it was well over that.

People must wonder how a physician can occasionally jump at a diagnosis and be right about it. Usually it is because we have seen something like it before. It is never exactly the same, mind you. There never are two cases in medicine exactly alike. But it can be near enough to strike some chord of memory. Let me illustrate.

Many years ago I was called to the apartment of a man on his return from four weeks spent in a medical center. When

I entered the room he was standing propped against a table
and grasping the seat of his trousers. The sweat of agony was
on his face, and there was the usual coterie of anxious female
relatives hovering about. So I asked the man how much
brandy he drank. The reaction was instantaneous and remarkable.

He swept some books off the table, danced on them in
rage, and shouted:

"Of course, I've drunk cognac, a bottle a day, for years.
Those fools at the hospital asked me about every kind of
alcohol but cognac and I told them no. They said I had
neuritis in my tail from arsenic in green vegetables. And
you've just been here thirty seconds and ask me about brandy."

What the man didn't know was that when I was a youngster
in Brittany years before I had treated an old peasant who was
notorious for the amount of crudely distilled wine he could
consume. Eventually nature caught up with him and alcoholic neuritis would make him lean against a table, grasping
the region of his anus and complaining of fearful bearing-
down pain. That picture had stuck in my memory. Brandy is
a curious beverage. Following such abuse, the drinker can be
out on his feet and give the general appearance of being as
sober as a judge. And there may be little or no odor of fusel
oil on his breath. They are bad drinkers, the brandy addicts.

The poor fellow in the apartment was willing to follow
the prescribed course. He quit cognac and with appropriate
medication was free from pain in two months. Then he
shifted to sherry, which is worse. But the treatment of alcohol addiction in the true chronic alcoholic is unimportant.
Nature has to have various ways of eliminating certain in-
dividuals. Alcohol is unfortunately slow but certain.

Now to get back to my architect stretched out on the floor
of his office. I asked him when he had suffered a previous

similar attack. He said, "Three months ago." Then I asked, "Did you eat chocolate that time and for lunch today?" He said, "Yes, chocolate ice cream." So that was it.

Shock tissue in the pacemaker of the heart had been irritated by the chocolate, inducing something called auricular flutter. If the flutter persists long enough the heart can dilate under the strain. Usually medication and a little time breaks the flutter and the heart goes back to regular rate and rhythm. This was so with the architect and he was told to report to the office for a thorough checkup.

There his history and physical examination proved interesting. A grandfather had a skin disease called psoriasis and had been crippled with arthritis early in life. That was probably called psoriatic arthropathica and is a classic allergic disorder. One of the patient's redheaded children had developed heart trouble after rheumatic fever. One had been treated for pulmonary tuberculosis. And a third child had a constantly wet nose and postnasal drip. The history seemed definite enough.

For some unknown reason medical practice seems to show that most blondes and practically all redheads have allergy.

Physical examination of the patient revealed a marked loss of vision in one eye, a condition that had existed since birth. His teeth were extremely irregular. For some unknown reason the more physical irregularities you are born with, the more likely you are to be artistic and allergic. The back of his neck and his back were covered with the silvery scars of an old pustular acne in childhood. X ray of the chest revealed a normal-sized heart and an old healed minimal amount of pulmonary tuberculosis. One leg was badly scarred where an attack of phlebitis had necessitated incision and drainage of an abscess. The patient was wearing narrow pointed shoes, so I asked him to remove his shoes and socks. His toes were practically crumbling away under the attack of a ringworm infection called athlete's foot. Great soggy masses of dead skin were peeling away between his toes. Because it didn't itch or give rise to pain, he had disregarded the condition, and the surgeon had not remarked upon it when he was under treatment for phlebitis. His main trouble was with his shoes. Many people have completely closed minds as to what they wear on their feet.

The results of the examination called for a carefully dictated letter which he could study at home.

"Dear Mr. De Muth:

"You have a diagnosis of:

"1. Allergy manifested by (a) the family history, (b) the pustular acne in childhood, (c) paroxysmal auricular flutter, (d) a small amount of old healed pulmonary tuberculosis, (e) extensive athlete's foot.

"The heart condition doesn't amount to much. That is merely a matter of avoiding chocolate in all forms now and forever. At the same time it is usually worth while to avoid the other common causes of allergic reactions: milk, cream, cheese, ice cream, eggs, wheat, and a second two-ounce drink of strong alcohol in twenty-four hours.

"Allergic people tend to die of pneumonia, so that it will probably be worth your while to be vaccinated against milk peptone every three years. That seems to protect against lobar pneumonia. Remember the date it is to be repeated.

"As I said, the heart condition isn't important but the neglected athlete's foot can kill you. I've already seen two deaths from secondary phlebitis because of it, and I don't want any more.

"Secondary infection from neglected athlete's foot can spread up into the veins in your legs. That means an attack of phlebitis. Correct treatment of phlebitis involves putting a kitchen chair on the foot of the bed, with the legs of the chair turned away from you. Up the back of the chair three pillows are placed in position. You have to lie in that position with both feet elevated at least two feet above your head until such time as gravity drainage helps to clear up the infection. With any injury or infection in the lower extremities this helps a great deal. Professional athletes are silly when they continue to limp around on a sprained ankle or a swollen knee. They should just lie with their feet up until the trouble is over.

"Your athlete's foot is bad enough to justify lying in this position for ninety minutes once a day, from 8 P.M. to 9:30 P.M. Each drainage period should last one hour and a half.

"With mild injury or infection of the lower extremities you drain once a day. Moderate injury or infection requires two ninety-minute drainage periods a day, and when it is severe three drainage periods a day are indicated.

"It is a curious thing in this life that practically no one appreciates the importance of downhill drainage when the lower extremities are in trouble. It takes what almost amounts to an act of God to get the nurses to give up their lovely special foot-rest elevators in hospital beds and resort to a kitchen chair and pillows, when lower extremities are in trouble. Such patients should have their feet high up and the special hospital beds are inadequate.

"You happen to be a rather long-lived type of individual. Every morning for the rest of your life I want you to put each foot on the washbowl in the bathroom. With your bare index finger scrub hard between all toes with ordinary soap and water. Plain tincture of green soap which you buy by the pint is perhaps as good as any when it comes to soap.

"Then you will have to learn how to buy shoes. Remember that I stood you on a piece of paper and drew an outline of your foot. Almost all foot troubles like bunions and corns and plantar warts and athlete's foot are due to bad shoes. I told you that you were wearing a stylish shoe exactly the width of your foot, 3 14/16 inches.

"Men wear extension soles and to get over athlete's foot your shoes must be 8/16 of an inch wider than your foot when you stand up with weight on your foot. This increased width of the sole, measured straight across, allows air to get between your toes. Air kills the ringworms. So from now on never go in a shoe store to buy shoes without a ruler in your pocket. As a class, shoe clerks seem to encourage people to buy shoes as narrow and as pointed as possible, and you need to buy shoes one half inch wider than your feet and with a rounded toe. Usually you ask for an army or navy officer's shoe. If you went on duty in the army with the kind of shoe you are wearing at present the adjutant would send you home to get properly dressed. There is nothing in nature that looks like a pointed shoe. Refuse them. Your foot is exactly 3 14/16 inches wide. Refuse to try on any shoe that isn't 4 6/16 inches wide straight across the sole. The letters A B C D E and EE mean nothing. A "B" width shoe in one type can be wider than an "EE" in another. You might ask for a AAA shoe 4 6/16 inches wide. That will really disconcert the shoe clerk and you may get co-operation. The poor women are really up against it. When they go into a shoe store and ask for a wide shoe they are practically shown to the door. Because so many women wear pumps one half inch narrower than their feet and because two out of three people have allergy, it seems to be true in the great cities that two out of three women have athlete's foot.

"Standing in chlorinated water in a gymnasium or locker

room is of no particular help. Be careful about salt-water bathing. The beach seems to be a favorite place for phlebitis to start up.

"There must be at least one thousand remedies that slightly modify athlete's foot. After their use the ringworms seem to take on increased resistance and remain in a low-grade state ready to attack any time that your feet perspire. The leather in your shoes has been heavily infected with ringworms. The smart thing to do is to get rid of the whole lot of them. Even leaving them out in the hot sunshine for a couple of months does no good. As to the rest of your routine, remember that allergy doesn't require a diet, but just the most perfect living you can achieve. A limit of eight hours in bed. Thirty minutes to clean in between your toes and shave and dress. Thirty minutes to walk without stopping. Thirty minutes to dawdle over a good breakfast and a good newspaper. Then go to work.

"The most perfect combination of food I know of consists of three meals a day of:

"1. One half pound of any good-tasting fresh meat with enough fat on it so that bowels move once a day.

"2. White or sweet potato or rice or yellow vegetable.

"3. Raw fruit other than apples, strawberries, tomatoes, oranges, or peaches, or any canned fruit you want.

"4. And a demitasse of black coffee.

"On such food you should have no more trouble with your heart."

But the architect did have another attack. Four months later at a dinner party he forgot and ate a creamy dessert with some flakes of bitter chocolate in it. Apparently for the last time he disgraced himself. I don't believe he will ever risk it again. For a week or two after starting treatment he was quite ashamed of his navy officer's shoes. But having two big corns disappear and the ringworm clear up has reconciled him to wearing them.

Almost all of the skin diseases may be benefited by the treatment of allergy. The severe chronic skin diseases in a charity hospital represent a great economic loss. Some of the patients have been in the wards for twelve or fifteen years at the cost to the city of ten to sixteen dollars a day. It might be a sensible idea to try feeding such cases one half pound of fresh fat meat without salt, and potato without butter, and canned pears three times a day. In the long run it could save a lot of time and money. But the skin men would first have to become more skeptical of skin testing and of temporary improvement from hormone therapy.

If the sum total of human knowledge could be added to in one small respect it would seem to justify existence. I would be satisfied with my life if I could just get people to wash their feet every morning and buy decent shoes.

Chapter XVII

VULNERABLE BLOOD VESSELS

THE TELEPHONE rang at ten o'clock one night with a request to hurry over to the banquet hall of a hotel where one of the officers of an engineering society had suffered a stroke. I found a forty-year-old man stretched out on the floor of the dais surrounded by his anxious friends. His color was good and there were no signs of paralysis. He complained of a dreadful whirling dizziness and if he turned his head as little as one inch he would have projectile vomiting that shot out six feet.

The story was not uncommon. Three banquet martinis (the lowest form of alcoholic life), then oysters, and a dinner winding up with chocolate ice cream. Ten minutes later the crash had come and he slid to the floor. I had seen something like it before and told his friends that the condition, allergic cerebellar angiospasm, was not serious and a few days would fix him up. The first move was getting him into the hospital.

The next morning a more careful history and physical examination elicited some pertinent facts. Two of his grandparents had suffered with some sort of chronic skin trouble. His father got hives whenever he ate strawberries or tomatoes or peaches. As a child the patient had a running ear which had continued to discharge periodically ever since. He was a little deaf in that ear in consequence. Migraine attacks had interfered with studying ever since his college days. He had had puffs under his eyes for as long as he could remember. Three years before he had been told that occasional attacks of dizziness which bothered him were due to Menière's disease and that nothing could be done about it. Physical examination showed only the puffs under the eyes, a little discharge of pus from his right ear, and difficulty in balancing while walking. Then too he was twenty pounds overweight. It wasn't a bad setup at all, and I could afford to be cheerful.

He was told the diagnosis of Menière's disease was out of the picture because that involved jerky involuntary movements of the eyeball and persistent dizziness, something he did not have. He would have to remain in the hospital a few more days until he could walk straight. In the meanwhile, he would be fed nothing but boiled rice and hot water. During this time, I wanted to rule out two possibilities. An old abscess in a mastoid could account for periodic discharge from the ear and for the vomiting. I didn't think it was probable but the mastoid area should be X-rayed to make sure. Then, headaches in the back of the head could be due to gallstones. Many years before, my foot had slipped on that diagnosis. After two months of my futile treatment for migraine, John Erdmann, the surgeon, had cured a woman's headaches by removing a gall bladder full of stones. I never wanted to be caught that way again, so even though I was pretty certain it would probably show nothing, a gall bladder X ray with dye was taken. Both of the X rays were negative. By the time this was over the patient could walk straight and was told that his treatment was more suitable for office practice than it was for hospital care. He was discharged and given an office appointment and asked to bring his wife with him because the treatment was involved and her co-operation essential.

In the office the lady proved to be what the French call *formidable*. It was plainly going to be a battle, so I asked the secretary not to disturb me for a half hour. The wife had a huge frame, a square jaw, and apparently was the kind of a woman who goes around putting everyone on committees. She was volubly blaming herself for her husband's trouble. She hadn't stopped his cigarettes in time and she couldn't get him to take his vitamins. He worked much too hard. She had fed him orange juice, whole wheat cereal with cream, protein bread toast, bacon and eggs, and synthetic coffee for breakfast. At night she usually gave him canned soup, which he liked, chicken and lots of green vegetables, a tossed salad and layer cake. He wouldn't take vitamins even though she kept them on the table.

The war was on when I told her that the diagnosis of allergic cerebellar angiospasm meant that her husband had inherited shock tissue in the blood vessels of his hind brain. The blood vessels went into a cramp when he ate bad food. He would have to live on simple old-fashioned food until such time as he had received nine injections of foreign protein and his body weight was normal.

What did I mean when I said bad food? What good were injections? His present weight looked just right to her. The idea of setting an alarm clock to get up in the morning was particularly silly. Her husband got his best sleep in the morning.

But a physician mustn't let a petty tirade disturb him, even though I had just seen the contrast of some pure unalloyed heroism in the next room.

For twenty years I had fought to keep a nice girl functioning in spite of a lot of trouble. Her husband and her sons adored her. Five years before a breast had had to come off for cancer. Then a severe sciatica made it necessary to get some X rays of the spine. She and her husband had come in to get the report, which gave the worst possible news. Extensive destruction of the spine from a spreading cancer was evident.

I must be a poor poker player indeed because the grief I felt showed through, and a lame explanation about arthritis didn't go over at all.

She leaned over and took her husband's hand to say, "Now look, Doctor, you stop worrying. I know it's cancer and all I want you to do is to make me comfortable. I've had a simply wonderful life and I don't want to live forever, particularly if I can't get well."

Talk about courage! Some of us humans can rise to the heights with the eagles.

But to get back to the work of explaining to the other woman what I wanted. Like many of the laity, she had no appreciation of the problems that confront physicians.

If her husband's way of living was to be straightened out, it was essential to have her co-operation. That was the one thing to keep in mind. There is an old military axiom that when you are in trouble it is better to attack. So I fired both barrels.

"In the first place keep this in mind. If your husband has more than one inch of loose fat on his lower abdomen, measured between fingers, expect him to die fifteen years before his appointed time. You won't enjoy life as a widow. For that reason I want you to keep flour off the table.

"People on ordinary mixed American food have almost no deficiencies that can be corrected by feeding vitamins. You would have to go to Asia or Africa to find many people who could be improved by vitamins.

"As far as cigarettes go, they seem only to be a pleasant bad habit. Smoked in moderation, they may be expensive but they do keep people from feeling lonely. The possibility that tar and other chemicals in them induces cancer of the lung is remote. Doctors familiar with the problem are far more worried about the tar inhaled on the roads during automobile travel.

"Irritating 'new' food and drink are cramping the blood vessels in your husband's brain. Some American men are being slowly slaughtered by lazy and ignorant housewives.

"Don't worry about his work. I have yet to see anyone die of overwork. It is extremely hard to work too hard. Most of his exhaustion comes from social activities.

"I want you to go to work in the kitchen and prepare some decent food. His organs have been breaking down steadily since he was thirty-three years old. They need to be repaired every day with something called amino acids which are present in fresh fat meat. See that you prepare in an attractive way one half pound of fresh fat meat for breakfast and dinner. Then try to persuade him to spend some money on fresh fat meat for lunch.

"Serve potato or rice or yellow vegetables in any way that tastes good as soon as his weight is normal. At the same time serve good raw and canned fruit. Until he has one inch of loose fat on his lower abdomen he can't have anything to eat but a big T-bone steak and a demitasse three times a day. After that you can expand his food a lot.

"While you are reducing your husband's weight to normal,

it might be an excellent idea to do the same thing yourself.

"Share with him the thirty-minute walk before breakfast, six glasses of water, and a big fat steak and a demitasse three times a day."

Rather to my amazement, and perhaps because I had just outtalked her, she agreed to try.

A couple of years later the husband and wife came in from Chicago. The man had never forgotten the terror of that night at the banquet. He had brought his weight down to normal and kept it there. With walking and good food his migraine and dizziness had been kept away. Even the ear had stopped discharging. The puffs under the eyes (a form of giant hives) would never be better because the skin had been stretched too long. But he had learned a lot about the gentle art of living well.

The report on his wife was not so good. She had stuck to her steak and demitasse until she lost twenty pounds. Then she had lost interest and regained it all. She had a question to ask. "The girls at my club are all taking some powder in a glass of water four times a day when they want to lose weight. Some of them say they lose eleven pounds in two weeks. Is that safe?"

So you tell her that nine-hundred-calorie crash diets are a recent vogue. The usual components of chocolate and soybean meal cloy the appetite but can give rise to severe allergic disorders. The lack of bulk frequently gives rise to obstinate constipation and gastric upsets. Just as with any other low-calorie diet, weakness and hunger and boredom result in the weight that is lost being regained with interest. Such food is lacking in many of the essential amino acids which are constantly present in fresh fat meat. and which are so essential to repair the daily wear and tear of cells in the heart and liver and arteries and in the stomach and intestines. If the only goal in weight reduction is to wear a smaller dress two weeks from now, it might be more efficiently accomplished by just taking lots of water. But starvation never has been and never will be safe.

Chapter XVIII

"MADISON AVENUE"
ULCER

THE PATIENT was tall. Slumped down in the examining chair, he presented a picture of abject despair. During the ten minutes that elapsed before I could see him he had chain-smoked two cigarettes and had telephoned twice to his office.

The chief complaint was of utter and complete exhaustion and that, generally speaking, life was a bust.

"Why is it a bust?" I inquired.

The response was, "I'm a lonely man in spite of a wife and three children. I work hard and when I get home at night over in Jersey the house is dark and there isn't a living soul to greet me."

My query was, "What time do you get home?"

"Oh, it might be three or four o'clock in the morning if I'm working late," he answered.

All the consolation he got out of that was my suggestion that if I happened to be his wife I'd greet him, probably with a baseball bat.

He took that in good part and the questioning proceeded.

He had no exact knowledge of his grandparents.

His father was master of hounds in a town in Virginia, and drank heavily enough to get occasional attacks of gout. Some purely allergic forms of gout do exist. The great toe joints swell up and become red and painful after things like orange juice, or alcohol, or cream, or coffee.

His mother dabbled in poetry, which was only published in the local newspaper. It is a curious thing how commonly worth-while artistic endeavor receives financial reward. Any artist should suspect that he or she is third rate if no one will pay for the product. And no one will ever tell the poor souls that their work is bad. Telling them that is supposed to kill something called the "spirit," so that they struggle on and on, often to the detriment of the usual number of children who lack shoes for school.

The patient had been glad to leave Virginia and go away to college because his father insisted on making a horseman of him, and he never felt at ease on horseback.

I told him the old tale about the hunt breakfast in Virginia. A New Yorker who was invited down for one such affair discovered that the girl on his right and the girl on his left talked horse in front of him and in back of him all through the repast. Finally one of the girls was remorseful and turned to him in apology.

"You know," she said, "we're all frightfully interested in hunting down here. What sport are you fond of?" "I shoot," he said. "What do you shoot?" she inquired. "Horses," he answered.

That cheered the patient up a bit and he went on with his story. All through college a wet nose had annoyed him. Alcohol gave him a terrible hangover. He snored so badly that no one would room with him, and for one period of two years giant hives had been a plague. On graduation from college he had joined a big advertising firm in which he had prospered. But starting an advertising campaign was an arduous task and he felt a chronic sense of exhaustion which he tried to relieve by attending numerous cocktail parties. A rather large house was needed to accommodate the family. His snoring was so bad that his wife used a separate bedroom so that she could get some sleep.

Physical examination showed a six-foot, two-inch individual, somewhat underweight, and with the big pupils, irregular teeth, markedly bent-in breastbone, and cold blue hands that denote a sensitive nervous system. It was not at all the type that goes hell for leather over the jumps on a fox hunt. I could see why his father despaired of him. But he was beautifully cast for the advertising business. In my experience that usually requires a solid compact individual at the head of the firm. Mercilessly he drives the well-educated, high-strung, irregular youngsters in the organization so that the deadline can be met. As a rule a girl has her work cut out for her if she marries one of these men in the advertising world. They seem to be as temperamental as quicksilver. Probably the reason for it is this: To be successful in the advertising business it is necessary to catch the public eye. That is a mild form of exhibitionism of which there are all grades. The most marked form of exhibitionism is one of the embarrassing things that can happen to an inspection party going through a state hospital for the insane. Owing to mental derangement, a few of the women patients may lift their skirts and the men drop their trousers. Some degree of modesty is always an accompaniment of normal behavior.

The patient was told that his main trouble was the underlying allergy manifested by the history of a wet nose, depression after excessive intake of alcohol, snoring, and giant hives. The sense of exhaustion in some way was connected with the hives, which are probably incurable. There is no proof of it but internal hives seems to be the best explanation of chronic sense of exhaustion.

He should watch closely to see if the wet nose and the snoring and the sense of exhaustion sharply decreased five days after starting anti-allergic treatment.

That involved complete and immediate deprivation of milk, cream, cheese, ice cream, chocolate, eggs, wheat flour, and alcohol. He was required to stay in bed eight hours or less, but there must be no hurry in the morning. Time must be allotted for a thirty-minute walk outdoors before breakfast. Each meal should consist of one half pound of fresh fat meat, potato with salt butter, canned fruit with the juice of one half of a fresh grapefruit in it when possible, and a demitasse of black coffee with plenty of sugar. He needed a snack of a big bowel of rice or tapioca pudding before retiring. Six glasses of water should be drunk in the office.

He was told that his employer would respect him more if he had a clean desk at five o'clock and then quit for the day. The world was full of slaves who prided themselves on working overtime. If he wanted to prove himself to be executive timber he had better start working reasonable hours.

Vaccination with foreign protein was started and he was told to come in three times a week until the nine injections were finished.

Four days later an excited individual burst into the office. "My wife says that she blesses your name because I didn't snore at all last night," was his remark. His nose was dry and the sense of exhaustion had lessened. He was so enthusiastic that I couldn't help wondering how long he would be able to sustain the effort of good living. But it lasted for quite a while.

Then one morning at ten minutes of eight I found him

pacing up and down in front of the office building awaiting my arrival. A tremendously important thing had happened. In order to finish up some sort of a rush job he and his secretary had worked steadily for two days and nights. Then at four o'clock in the morning he happened to look over at her. She was misty-eyed and a halo of bright light seemed to be around her head. Without further ado he said, "I love you." She murmured, "I love you too." So they went out to Child's and discussed their future over pancakes and coffee. He told her that his physician was a real friend and that his advice was needed. And here he was.

Impulsively I reached for my wallet and gave him all the money I had on me. "This is serious business," I said, "and only time and reflection can solve the problem. Take this money and save out only twenty-five dollars. Go down to Grand Central Station. With the rest of the money buy a ticket and a Pullman berth as far west as you can get. When you get off the train call me up long distance and I'll tell you what to do next. It has been my experience that promiscuous love affairs only turn out well in books and magazines. In real life they wind up in divorce with alimony, or pregnancy, or a venereal disease, or the worst of all, which is mental pain. You need some time. Lots of time. Now get going."

Fervidly wringing my hand, he departed. The telephone call never came in.

A week later a shamefaced man stood before me. It seemed that on the way down to Grand Central he had met a bachelor friend from the office. Bursting with the news, he had told him about the glorious thing that had happened. The friend said that the doctor was all wrong. This was the kind of real romantic love that couldn't possibly happen but does. He should do the natural thing and go get the girl. The key to his friend's apartment was proffered and accepted.

The immediate trouble was complete disillusionment, based upon the discovery of an acutely painful form of venereal disease. Then came the job of getting a bed in the hospital. Oh well! Life is like that. A physician can't help trying to reline people's brakes, futile as it may seem at times.

Ten years elapsed before the man showed up again, after being fixed up in the hospital. In the meantime he had become careless about living and an annoying chronic indigestion made him accept a friend's suggestion to go to a great diagnostic clinic for a complete checkup. There not a soul had asked him about a wet nose or snoring or hives or sense of exhaustion, which is routine. Hardly anyone asks the right questions about allergy. After a gastrointestinal X-ray series the patient was told that he had a duodenal ulcer that required immediate treatment with frequent feedings of milk and eggnog and custard. A lot of medicine was given him. The patient was warned that an operation on his stomach might be inevitable.

Following this treatment, the patient was worse in every respect and had come in to see me about having an operation.

Another gastrointestinal X ray showed a markedly deformed duodenum with what might be an ulcer niche. The X-ray man made a positive diagnosis of ulcer. But one film of the duodenum showed a large-sized bulb, and an ulcer usually causes permanent shrinkage and clover-leaf deformity. There was no retention in the stomach past the usual time of emptying. Ulcer usually causes such a retention. The patient had never hemorrhaged and an ulcer usually bleeds. So he was told that the clinical diagnosis was allergic functional pylorospasm and that he needed the same treatment for allergy which had been used for his wet nose and snoring and sense of exhaustion. His latest problem was just another form of the same thing.

Back he went on the original routine with the same improvement noted four days later.

During the eight years he has remained under observation since then he has been symptom-free and sticks faithfully to his routine. The snoring stopped again and his nose is dry. Every three years he repeats his series of injections. A while ago he told me that his experiences in living as a young man just seemed like a bad dream. The family is a happy one and that is the main thing about being a physician. Somehow or other you may be able to keep the family on an even keel.

Too many people who work on Madison Avenue brag about having an ulcer. All that may be needed is good living.

Chapter XIX

FOOD, GOOD, BAD,
AND INDIFFERENT

WE HUMANS have always been and always will be interested in two vital things: food and reproduction. In this
country food and reproduction seem to be quite similar in two
respects—the quantity is too high and the quality too low.

Any consideration of food sets one right back on the heels
of comparative anatomy. Up to eight thousand years ago the
fuel we consumed was ideal for the design of our bodies. Design is mainly shown by the length of a bowel and the shape
of the teeth. A herbivorous animal like a cow or a horse or a
sheep has a monstrous length of bowel, perhaps twenty-six
times the length of its spine, with teeth that are modified for
grinding. The plant food that is ingested has cellulose as a
framework, and there is no juice in the body of anything living
that will split cellulose to liberate its food value. So that
cellulose has to be broken down under bacterial action. The
great length of bowel offers an ideal manure pile where the
bacteria can go to work. A purely carnivorous animal, such
as a lion, has a short bowel, only nine times the length of

the spine. He doesn't have to bother with much cellulose digestion. The human bowel is about sixteen times the length of the spine, and human teeth are modified for some grinding, so that the primitive food we lived on for millions of years suited us exactly. Our inclination goes far toward the carnivora, regardless of the opinion of the vegetarians.

Then too we know that all cells in the body have qualities in common. If the best food to preserve our teeth could be discovered we would probably have the best food to preserve all the rest of our organs. And what has been observed about teeth?

It is certain that many of us inherit an enamel on our teeth which is too soft to prevent dental decay. People with soft teeth have been urged for many years to consume large quantities of milk and cod-liver oil and green vegetables in the effort to "increase the calcium and vitamin D." The fact that the treatment does not work never seems to occur to anyone. The more you take of these things the bigger the dental bills become. And candy seems to raise the very devil. The worst teeth in the world are seen in Scotland where oatmeal seems to suck something out of the enamel. No! If you want to have strong jaws and teeth that are much less subject to dental caries it is better to live on primitive food. The regular cleaning of teeth helps a lot too.

It is always interesting to observe the cussedness in human nature. A heavy manual laborer, such as a ditch digger, with a loaf of bread and an onion for lunch is well fed. Such food furnishes the energy for hard work. Whereas a banker, who it is fervently hoped is doing a lot of thinking, needs a sirloin steak and half of a grapefruit and a demitasse. You can think all day and not get fat on that kind of food.

One thing that must always be kept in mind about food is

that "All flesh is grass." A walrus rips up the ocean bottom to get at clams. If he can get enough of them he can keep in good condition. But the clams depend mainly upon vegetable matter in the water for their well-being. The animals convert the starchy vegetables into the sorely needed protein and fat that we humans crave.

Water remains the most necessary food in both the vegetable and the animal kingdoms.

From the good earth come the nitrogen and potash and phosphorus which, after water, are the main requirements in plant feeding. These contain the small amounts of the trace minerals and vitamins essential to proper growth. In parts of the deep South it has been shown that magnesium is in deficient supply. Magnesium is one of the elements present in the all-important chlorophyll of plants. Adding magnesium to the soil converts it into splendid farming country. And up in the North country there may be a deficiency in boron in the land, in which case, and unless the soil is reinforced, the apple orchard will be a failure. The farmers all know that in some parts of the country it is impossible to raise certain crops such as good pears or peaches or lima beans or onions. The chemists are not yet expert enough to tell what is lacking in the soil.

The same sort of thing exists in the animal kingdom, where protein, fat, and carbohydrate are the three main food requirements. Almost all fresh foods contain small amounts of other essential organic substances needed to permit utilization of food and to maintain health and promote growth. These substances are called vitamins and act as catalysts, things that act in a mysterious way by reason of their presence. A long list of diseases have been proven to be due to an absence or decreased amount of vitamins, or to the body's failure to utilize them when abundant. However, the food in the United States of America is in such generous supply that only in rare instances do we see evidence of true vitamin deficiency or encounter any disease that can be corrected by feeding vitamins. The vitamin business in this country is simply an excellent way to keep the money of credulous people in circulation. That is a pretty broad statement and I had better attempt to justify it.

I had an unparalleled opportunity to try out vitamin therapy for many years in a great charity hospital. Many of the patients were derelicts who had lived for years on the worst kind of alcohol and baker's bread. A few of them developed scurvy or the type of painful neuritis that follows prolonged alcoholic debauches. Curing the scurvy or neuritis with vitamins enabled them to go out and drink some more. Cheilosis, an inflammation around cracks in the corners of the mouth, can be due to vitamin deficiency. But there are other causes and most commonly nothing would help but good dentures. Shiny tongues and painful calf muscles were not uncommon, but if we had nerve enough to sign a patient out with "death from vitamin deficiency" the autopsy would show a cancer that was not connected with a hollow organ and which had been missed in diagnosis. The poison of the cancer had prevented the proper utilization of good food.

Once we observed a woman pellagra victim from the deep South who had been living on nothing but hominy grits. Corn is not a complete food because the zein in it is deficient in the essential amino acids tryptophan and lysine. She had a craving for the tar on the inside of a chimney that served a wood-burning stove. It was small wonder that she would expectorate all day long until the anti-pellagra vitamin brought her under control. And that was about the sum total as far as improving sick people with vitamins went. We do see nowadays the rare case of pernicious anemia that is kept in good condition with the vitamin B_{12}. And once in a while, and in patients over the age of sixty-five, B_{12} injections give a transient sense of well-being.

But, generally speaking, vitamin therapy in this country is a branch of ornithology. It is for the birds. It might work well in a prison camp in Asia or Africa.

After water, perhaps the most needed thing in good nutrition is an adequate intake of amino acids. Animal proteins, except for gelatine, contain the ten essential amino acids needed for growth or repairing tissue waste.

One of the kings of France thought that a cheap way of feeding his soldiers had been discovered in gelatine, but gelatine is lacking in eleven different amino acids. The soldiers became sick.

First-class proteins, such as meat, contain all of the essential amino acids, while second-class proteins like those in wheat and corn lack some of them. One of the reasons that physicians may dislike feeding wheat flour to allergics could be its extremely high content of glutamic acid and the complete lack of lysine. Proper growth does not occur in the absence of lysine. It may be possible in the future to produce lysine in commercial quantities at a reasonable price. Then our stored surplus wheat could be reinforced with it and fed to animals able to convert wheat into the wanted fat and protein.

The indispensable amino acids which must be present in food are ten in number and are called essential. The others can be built up in the body from various components and are called non-essential. It might be well to list the table made out by Rose in experimental work on rats.

Essential	Non-essential
Arginine	Alanine
D- or L-Histidine	Aspartic acid
D-Isoleucine	Citrulline
L-Leucine	Cystine
D-Lysine	Glutamic acid
L-Methionine	Glycine
D- or L-Phenylalanine	Hydroxyglutamic acid
D-Threonine	Hydroxyproline
D- or L-Tryptophan	Norleucine
D-Valine	Proline
	Serine
	Tyrosine

Apparently—I repeat—there are only two absolutely necessary foods for humans—fresh fat meat and water. The longest I have ever kept anyone on that food exclusively is nine months. That was with a patient who was monstrously overweight, but at the end of that time he showed no evidence of any mineral or vitamin deficiency and was in excellent condition.

Protein furnishes heat and is essential for the repair of the wear and tear of tissues. In a state of maximum growth protein cannot be stored. All of the nitrogen taken in as protein in food will be turned out within twelve to sixteen hours, but fat and carbohydrate, if not used for muscular work, can be stored as adipose tissue. Fat is much superior to starch as a fuel. It burns with a clear hot fire and doesn't leave clinkers as does starch. But the womenfolks are annoyed when the butcher doesn't trim off a lot of extra fat from the meat. And that is unfortunate.

What are the theoretical and practical objections to those seven foods that seem bad for most cases of eczema and other allergic disorders?

Milk, if in adequate quantity, is an ideal nursing infant

food when taken through a teat from a similar animal. Taken from a different animal and preserved in a bottle, it can be one of the most heavily infected and irritating foods there is, regardless of the pearly-white color. Pasteurization, when enforced, has been a Godsend in the prevention of intestinal and glandular tuberculosis in children. But that seems to be about the only infection that is controlled by it, and there are many others. Heating cow's milk long enough, as in evaporated and condensed and dried milk, can destroy enough of the irritating qualities to permit its use by some babies and children suffering from eczema. Others can't touch cow's milk in any form.

The same objections apply to cream, and that hellish combination that passes for cream in a cheap restaurant. Apparently that is a mixture of milk and gelatine and marshmallow, plus some weird chemicals. A dessert topped with real whipped cream could be a perfect explanation of a bout with undulant fever.

Cheese can have the same infections and irritants that are in milk. The worst cases of eczema I have ever seen were contracted in Yugoslavia where cheese was partaken of twice a day for a couple of months. The dreams of the rarebit fiend, made famous by Winsor McCay many years ago, were based on solid fact. Cheese eating can lead to wild dreams and even Indians in the North country seem to know that cheese constipates them.

Roquefort cheese, when made in the original manner from sheep's milk, is perhaps the least irritating of any. But now cow's milk is often substituted. Blindfolded, many people have difficulty in distinguishing between Stilton, Gorgonzola, Danish Blue, and New York State Roquefort. They all gain flavor by decomposition, and decomposition products can raise the devil with allergics. Modern factory methods of producing cheese in bricks which are easy to market, but are made of green cheese with a host of chemicals, seem particularly reprehensible.

Ice cream used to be one of my boyhood delights. Grandmother made it out of a cooked custard and her grandsons turned the crank of a ten-quart freezer. I was always allowed to have what adhered to the paddle when the ice cream became stiff. We never seemed to get sick from it, and it can still be made that way if anyone has the strength and the brains. Apparently cooking the custard was the answer. But nowadays ice cream, even though made in a factory that is so spotlessly clean you could eat off the floor, is usually made of raw ingredients. If any real cream is put in it, it may have been preserved for two years before use. All sorts of chemicals, many of which physicians have never even heard of, go into the preparation of modern ice cream and add to the velvety texture. The most recent effort of the ice cream chemists is to dispense with milk and cream entirely and use vegetable fats, which are whiter. The combination of cheap chocolate on the outside and bean dust on the inside for texture can keep children with asthma or hay fever or any other allergic manifestations in constant trouble.

Bitter chocolate is made by grinding roasted cocoa beans which have been freed from germ and shell. Sweet chocolate contains added sugar, and milk chocolate added sugar and dried milk. Cocoa is chocolate deprived of a portion of its fat and pulverized.

The eating and drinking of chocolate is perhaps the commonest and the best-known way to precipitate allergic troubles. Why it is, nobody knows, unless it is because it is derived from beans and most of the bean family are anathema in allergy.

Many people are aware of the way the body can resent egg

eating. Eggs can apparently precipitate migraine headaches, an attack of irregular gout, and make a lot of skin diseases worse. One of the best-tasting breakfast dishes there is may be a perfectly made omelet, but it doesn't agree with a lot of us. Again no one knows why. Perhaps it is the high peptone content.

Wheat flour is a fearfully concentrated food. It can furnish wonderful energy for muscular work in people who are thin or normal in weight. As a little boy I used to marvel at old George Booth in our town. He would consume thirty big pancakes for breakfast and then go out to plow furrows that were straight as a die, all day long. But that kind of work, and the need for such fuel, has gone out of style. No one knows whether the trouble with wheat in allergic disorders is due to the high glutamic acid content or the lack of lysine or some other factor. It seems almost impossible to make palatable breadstuff out of any other flour when used alone. Unless wheat flour is added the product becomes stale at once. Bread substitutes, when used for school luncheons, are lacking in flavor. Corn pone, slabs of corn meal mush, cream of rice mush, and cold fried sweet potatoes all involve a lot of cooking and suffer by comparison. But it is amazing at times to see how much more comfortable a patient with duodenal ulcer can be when wheat flour is withdrawn from the menu. Bread can give a lot of people a "sour stomach," and splitting headaches and joint pains and bad skins.

Beside the "big bad seven" there are other foods that may irritate our livers. "A jug of wine, a loaf of bread—and thou beside me singing in the wilderness," may be perfectly all right for one third of us, but the other two thirds who tend toward obesity and allergic disorders had better shy away from drinking. Alcohol is fearfully fattening for many of us. When a fat person is regularly losing weight at the rate of three pounds a week, on nothing but a big fat steak and a demitasse twenty-one times a week, it can be expected that one glass of beer will add one half pound to the body weight. A martini or a highball will add about one pound and a bacardi cocktail one and a quarter pounds. There is not much future in that. With allergic disorders alcohol can make the face of someone cursed with acne look as though it had been run over by a tractor. Hives, hay fever, asthma, sense of exhaustion, headaches, and digestive disturbances can all be made markedly worse by any form of alcoholic beverage.

Green vegetables can contain unknown irritants, aside from additive sprays, that bother some of us a great deal. Annoying intestinal gases or joint pains or sudden elevations of blood pressure may all stop when such patients are deprived of green vegetables. I have one family who love asparagus and have a big patch of it to feast on during the season. The whole family run elevated blood pressures at that time. There is a region in Italy where a certain kind of bean is popular as food. Everyone who eats the beans seems prone to increased blood pressure. Green vegetables have a high cellulose or roughage content. People who are nervous, or of advanced age, attribute tremendous importance to huge daily bowel movements like those of a horse or a cow. These they can obtain by eating a lot of green vegetables. But that isn't normal in a human. The bulky stools that follow the eating of green vegetables depend mainly for their weight on the bodies of dead and living bacteria that have been busy splitting cellulose.

We should be mainly carnivorous, and carnivorous animals have much smaller bowel movements and usually skip one or two days a week. There is no single trick that is much good for constipation. But if the general routine (adequate sleep, the thirty-minute walk, three big meals a day, six glasses of water, and enough fat on the meat) is adhered to, then accessory fat does help. Remember that we humans do better with smooth food than we do with roughage. Accessory fat can easily be put in by eating four fresh homemade sausage balls before dinner as canapés. The sausage is made up in an amount that will last only two days. Usually four big center-cut pork or veal chops are bought. The meat is cut off and mixed with a little salt and a lot of good pepper and sage. Then it is fried in balls about the size of big walnuts. Another good trick that results in freer elimination can be adapted from a custom used by the natives in the Hebrides. A pound of good white beef suet can be cut into small pieces and melted over low heat in a frying pan. The colorless liquid is stored in an empty container and kept in the icebox, where it can be expected to turn hard and white. Floating a tablespoon of that hard fat on a cup of hot coffee or tea and drinking it before going for the morning walk usually results in normal bowel movements. The taste is something like bouillon.

Adding parsley and celery leaves and onion to meat for flavoring seems unobjectionable and pleasant. So many people develop hives after eating raw oranges or strawberries or apples or tomatoes or peaches that it seems unwise for allergics to partake of them. Cooking usually destroys any irritating quality in these raw fruits, and it does the same for milk and cream when cooked for twenty-two minutes. There are plenty of other raw fruits to eat.

Food additives have become a tremendous problem for the investigators and for the public. Unless you raise your own vegetables and fruit and chickens and turkeys and pigs and bake your own bread you never know what you are eating nowadays. A mother may think she is feeding her child an ideal amount of vitamins with the green vegetables that she serves. As a matter of fact a test of the child's urine may show a large amount of arsenic or some other harmful spray. Up to a point the more spray the farmer uses to keep down loss from insect attack the prettier the crop. Apparently one careless farmer out in the West did some terrible damage. A town had an outbreak of what was diagnosed as a peculiarly fatal form of horse sleeping sickness and a great many people died. Then a smart physician remembered that arsenic has a marked affinity for the cells in the nervous system. Poisoning by arsenic can imitate many diseases involving the brain or spinal cord. Bodies of some of the victims were dug up and their brains were found to be dripping with arsenic. At the same time word came of a similar epidemic thought to be horse sleeping sickness in a town outside of Boston. The doctors there were advised to check for arsenic, with the same result. On reconstructing the disaster, it was thought probable that a carload of green vegetables had been split up. One half went to the West and one half to the East.

Perhaps the only reasonably safe spray that can be used with some effect on vegetables and fruit is pyrethrum, which is a form of chrysanthemum dust. That is a natural product. However, after it began to be used extensively, it was noted that flies and mosquitoes developed an increased resistance to it. Then the frantic race started for new and more potent chemicals.

Chickens and turkeys are filthy birds at best. Owing to a lack of inspectors and the greed of producers, some of the sanitary conditions in factories where chickens and turkeys are raised, or processed, or both, are appalling. Chickens may never see sunlight from the time they are hatched. Chickens and turkeys may be fed hormones and then soaked in an antibiotic after dressing. The hormones put on a little weight and the antibiotic enables the processor to store the fowl for a long time without the development of a rotten smell.

People complain that chickens and turkeys no longer have the flavor they used to have thirty years ago. There is no proof of this because there are no thirty-year-old birds to use for comparison. The best you can do is to raise your own, with access to sunshine and young sweet clover. Feed them plain corn and table scraps. After cooking in the same way as a purchased bird, run a blindfold test to see which is more palatable!

Even with a fast gain in weight and a cheap price, chicken is still exceedingly expensive. A costly six-pound roasting chicken may have only a pound and one half of available meat after cooking.

The five- or ten-gallon cans full of frozen cooked chicken à la king, or chicken salad, or creamed chicken that are brought into restaurants and then opened and served seem to be one of the easiest ways ever devised to guarantee food poisoning.

Perhaps five or ten per cent of meat animals are now being injected with hormones and the producers are stupid beyond words to do this. The gain in weight is slight at best and the public fear of cancer is universal. But the producers listen to the siren song of the big chemical companies.

There is no definite proof that hormones fed to animals pull the trigger on cancer in humans or cause perforated gastric ulcer or appendicitis or prevent the healing of wounds, although such disasters do occur when hormones are used in medicine.

I saw one case that seemed fairly definite. A patient with a bone cancer in the shoulder called myeloma was given hormones to allay severe pain. Within five weeks a full-blown carcinoma of the breast developed. That cured me, if not the patient.

Competition in the bakery business is terrific. Profit on a

loaf of bread is not estimated in pennies but in mills. Time was when one of the finest perfumes in a kitchen was that of a loaf of good home bread baking in the oven. The woman took great pride in the quality of a loaf even if it did get stale in twenty-four hours. The commercial bakers went to work on the women, utilizing the fact that most of us are just as physically and mentally lazy as we can be and get away with it. So with the aid of a horrifying number of chemicals, they baked a loaf of bread that was good-looking, in a spotlessly clean wrapper, and of even texture soft enough so that the fingers of the purchaser could meet in the middle ten days after baking. It was a real chemical triumph even if it wasn't worth a damn in a culinary sense. The last large firm to make good homemade bread in New York City has quit the struggle. To prevent their product from getting moldy, and normal bread should get moldy, they have added sodium propionate to it. No one knows whether sodium propionate can precipitate cancer or not. The safest rule is not to buy anything that contains it. Probably the worst of the chemical additives is monosodium glutamate, sometimes called glutamic acid or vegetable protein derivative. They are the same thing. They are hawked under other names. Whole cookbooks are written around the ability of monosodium glutamate to "flavor" food. Instead of flavoring, what it does is to irritate the wall of the stomach to a stage of bright red, acute congestion. The acute congestion causes a hunger sensation, so you ask for a second helping. The Japs sent shiploads of it to us before the last war in exchange for our scrap steel, and now great factories in this country perpetrate it upon the public. Most of the canned soup that you buy contains the miserable stuff. Manufacturers aren't particularly bright when they listen to their chemists. Once the public realizes that acute congestion of the stomach is an almost ideal way to induce cancer of the stomach in a susceptible individual, canned soups will change their ways.

Everyone these days seems to desire a refrigerator with adequate storage space for frozen foods. That is a good thing to have if you happen to be particularly fond of pork or if you live many miles away from a store where fresh food is sold. Freezing pork is just about as effective as heat in killing trichinae, the worms that produce "measly" pork, so you won't have to cook the pork to death to serve it in a palatable form. But the other foods—meat and fish and fruit and vegetables—all seem to suffer a loss in flavor when frozen.

Legend has it that the art of quick freezing was discovered by a drunken trapper in the far North. After a debauch he was out of food and had to gouge a hole through many feet of ice to catch fish. Even the arctic Eskimos hole up when the temperature is fifty degrees below zero, but he had to fish or die. The captured fish instantly froze when he dropped them on the ice. When he took them into his shack in a bucket containing snow and lit the fire to heat up the cabin, the snow in the bucket melted and the fish came to life and swam around. Apparently life was suspended by instant subjection to intense cold. The limiting membranes of the cells were not ruptured by the thawing of big ice crystals, which normally form in slow freezing. The idea was patented and sold for a great deal of money, and never used. It costs a little more to subject anything to intense cold, at forty degrees below zero. So commercial refrigeration is set at about twenty-eight degrees below zero. That is high enough so that when frozen food is thawed the limiting membranes of cells rupture as the big ice crystals melt and the flavor evaporates. Too, the greed of producers may enter into the indifferent quality of frozen foods. Fruits or vegetables or fish or meat that cannot be marketed for some reason or other may be frozen when quite stale. Freezing never does anything but detract from the original quality. If a housekeeper lives anywhere near a market that sells fresh food it seems better to buy it twice a week. For that length of time it keeps well in an ordinary refrigerator. Maybe some-day food at the peak of perfection will be frozen at forty degrees below zero, stored at exactly ten degrees above zero, and thawed out quickly under infra-red cold heat, and then cooked. Perhaps then it could be first class.

All over the world the people who market fish are in dire financial straits. One simple thing never seems to occur to them. People dislike poor fish and stale fish. A poor fish like red perch on the Grand Banks used to be dumped overboard when netted. Now it is frozen and sold as some-thing like ocean perch. Nothing deteriorates faster than fish or shellfish. Unfortunately fish may undergo perhaps fifty changes in temperature from the time it is caught until it is marketed, so that it is always desirable to at least buy fish that is in season. In New York City that means codfish and smelt in the wintertime. It has to be kept in mind that fish when it is stale, as manifested by dull eyes and pale gills, may be filleted, frozen, and kept indefinitely. If you are iodine- and fish-hungry in the wintertime it is better to buy a whole small codfish, called a scrod. If the eyes are bright and the gills the right color it is probably fresh. Then it can be filleted and skinned and it will be much better than any hatchery trout. The commercial fishermen usually pack fish in ordinary ice. That only drops the temperature as a rule to thirty-one degrees. Bacterial decomposition takes place at that temperature, along with the development of a stale smell and appearance. A brilliant engineer named Crosby Field may have developed a process that will revolutionize the fish industry. Ribbons of salt-water ice can now be made out of clean natural sea water or reinforced fresh water. Fish packed in this are reduced in temperature to twenty-eight degrees above zero. This is too low for most bacterial growth. The fish retain a fresh smell and appearance. Commercial application of the method is already in effect in Norway. We may soon see it used in this country. Fish are low in fat content, so that you can rapidly get hungry after a main meal of fish. Mackerel is the fattest fish, but there is a definite limit to the number of mackerel anyone can eat.

Enough of destructive criticism! It is too easy, and I like to do things the hard way. Let's talk about good food.

Chapter XX

THE SIMPLE LIFE

LET ME SAY now that I don't know the first single solitary thing about cooking.

But I wish more people would take pride in their work. Good cooking is an honorable estate, like holy matrimony. To me it seems a great art, and the determination of when heat should be lowered or raised the finest end point in chemistry. Some people have the ability to make things taste good, and others can't even boil water. Food that tastes good is much more likely to be well digested by the increased flow of gastric juice which attends good appetite.

What I do know is that a great deal of expensive food is partially ruined by last-minute cooking at high temperatures.

Long slow cooking of roast meats is not yet popular in this country, but if flavor and tenderness, with as little waste as possible, are desired, there seems to be no other method. It takes courage to put a roast of meat in the oven at noontime, with an accurate thermometer in the oven registering no higher than two hundred and fifty degrees. Before serving for dinner that night, the heat can be raised to brown the meat. The meat needs no basting and only a little is wasted in shrinkage. But women don't seem to trust their stoves to continue cooking at low heat while they are out of the house. Or they may not be home at noontime, and then may want to sit around and be sociable before the evening meal is announced. That calls for last-minute incineration of expensive steak or chops. However, the feelings of the little woman are more important than steak.

Next comes the question of other good food in these United States of America. If memory serves me right, for I can't find the quotation, a famous Frenchman, one Charles Maurice de Talleyrand-Périgord, told us exactly where we got off on that score. He returned to France with the comment that "American barbarians had thirty-two religions, and only one course for dinner."

M. de Talleyrand might feel that he was still right if he could see what an ordinary workingman and his family are commonly served for the evening meal. Sixty cents' worth of chemical cold cuts from the delicatessen is pretty poor fodder.

Life on the installment plan is precarious at best. The women feel the need to go out and earn money to help pay for aluminum storm windows. Something has to give, and it is usually the food and the children that suffer. It isn't smart to present a ten-year-old child with a house key. Children need a substantial snack when they come home from school, and someone to look after them. And everyone needs something decent to eat. Primarily that means enough fresh fat meat.

Boiling down to the economics as usual, let us consider the least expensive meat first, since ninety per cent of us have to worry about the cost of food.

In theory any fresh lean meat including fowl and fish works

if it is reinforced with fat. If you are particularly fond of chicken, and have no worries about it, breast of chicken can be ground up with enough flavoring and fresh beef suet to make excellent chickenburgers, or fresh fish or pork cracklings may be used. Cracklings are just pieces of beef or pork fat cooked down in a frying pan until about two thirds of the contained fat escapes, but not many people are fond of cracklings.

There is this to consider about any form of ground meat: the sharp oxygen attack that takes place ten minutes after meat is ground changes its color and flavor. Much research work is now going on in the effort to discover how oxygen attack can be prevented, but so far there is no solution. Four hours after grinding, even in an ordinary icebox or in the freezer, bacterial contamination goes to work. The sour taste of restaurant hamburgers, and of commercial sausages or prepared meats, is due to bacterial decomposition, or to the chemicals used to partially control it.

A housewife is unwise to stick her uncleaned meat grinder in the icebox the way the butchers do. They may only wash their grinders once a week in cold soda water. An uncleaned meat grinder can be a paradise for bacteria and give rise to a fearful attack of food poisoning.

Ground meat should be cut rather than crushed. Crushing meat ruptures the cell walls and allows the contained flavor to escape. And that is about all that Aunt Susy's dull old food chopper, which has been in the family for fifteen years and never been sharpened, accomplishes. By taking it apart to clean it twice during the operation, a dull hand grinder can be made to crush some meat but it is a real job to turn the handle. Even with power-driven meat grinders, many butchers subscribe to a service which furnishes them with sharpened blades once a week. Commercially there is available a new type of meat grinder with a raised blade that doesn't plug up with use. But the cost is around seven hundred dollars, which is completely out of the reach of most households. The meat-grinding attachments sold with some household electrical gadgets do not stand up to steady use. The armatures on the small motors burn out. But there is a heavy-duty small machine, which can be purchased for around thirty-seven dollars, that is a good job to use. This is particularly so if it is combined with a scale permanently attached to the kitchen table, one that weighs in ounces up to ten pounds. It is always smart to check the weight of meat purchased, and ground meat tastes better if the correct proportion of lean to fat (three parts lean to one of fat) is exactly adhered to. An additional advantage of a heavy-duty small electric meat grinder is that flavoring, such as celery leaves, parsley, onion, or cooked mushrooms, can be incorporated directly into the meat being ground.

Some households can't even afford a hand meat grinder, in which case it isn't desirable to buy the chopped meat which the butcher has already prepared in his showcase. That can have a red dye in it, or a cereal filler, and extra water for weight. It is better to ask him to grind to order six ounces of good white kidney suet and eighteen ounces of lean chuck. This can be divided into three cakes which make a quota for one person for three meals. The last two can't be expected to taste as good as the first, but the food value is there. Or a boned shoulder of lamb can be purchased. That contains about a correct proportion of fat and the meat can be ground as desired, or else cut off and broiled as lamb steaks.

Restaurants are in desperate need of some technological genius who can design a machine with inbuilt refrigeration that will deliver one quarter-pound portion of fresh fat meat ground to order. Two of those portions would make an adequate meal, and the meat would be fresh.

The less expensive cuts of meat require much more time and skill in preparation. Hash when prepared at home can be a culinary delight. Plenty of good fat cold roast beef or roast lamb can be ground or chopped with freshly boiled potato. Such onion and cooked mushroom and celery and parsley as is desired are added. Then it can be steamed in a covered fry pan or else browned.

A skilled mess sergeant knows that soldiers complain much less about food when they are given "slum" once a day. "Slum" is just good beef or lamb stew. It gains flavor by being kept over a day, but that can make it one of the finest ways there is to start an epidemic of dysentery among the troops. The combination of leftover meat and potatoes makes a happy hunting ground for bacteria, so only enough for one meal should be prepared.

A white lamb stew or a black beef stew can be a thing of beauty. Probably the black beef stew gains color by the addition of red wine and caramel. There is no objection to these flavorings unless an effort is being made to lose weight.

The Armenians know that the best-flavored lamb is found near the neck of the animal. One-and-a-quarter-inch cubes of boneless meat with plenty of attached fat can be cut from the neck, browned separately, and slowly cooked in olive oil until tender. When finished, freshly boiled carrots and potatoes and onions and celery can be added along with fresh parsley. There's a meal for champions. Forget the lamb and beef stew recipes in the cookbooks. They always call for lean meat with bones. The bones are just camouflage as far as weight of meat goes. They add next to nothing to flavor and make the meat difficult to eat. Any loose fat that rises to the top of the separately cooked meat cubes can be skimmed off in just about ten seconds. Recently I asked a fine Italian chef to prepare for me such a stew, using only cubes of fresh fat beef. He had no difficulty whatever in producing a masterpiece.

Because of the new knowledge about the importance of fat in meat, a great many cookbooks should be rewritten. For instance, consider pot roast. A fine meat, pot roast, but try to get a good one in any restaurant! What should happen is this: Six pounds of good lean meat is rolled and tied. Then, the butcher cuts through the strings to the center. Two pounds of kidney suet is placed in the gap. The butcher reties it. In such fashion the inside fat will not be cooked away. Slowly cooked with proper seasoning, and with a good gravy made with potato flour or potato starch (they are just the same), pot roast makes a grand meal, particularly when served with freshly made potato pancakes.

Boiled beef when correctly made of good fat brisket, as it is in Europe, is a first-class meal. I don't know what they do to it in this country. Perhaps it is boiled rather than simmered. And maybe they don't allow it to stand in the water it is cooked in long enough afterward to be juicy. Along with a good horse-radish sauce, it can be wonderful. Veal chops with part of a veal kidney incorporated in them can be a delightful adventure in eating. Slowly roasted fresh ham appeals at times. Unpeeled veal kidneys with the outside kidney fat left on can be simmered three times and the water discarded. Then quick broiling can result in marvelous flavor.

I learned to like boiled pigs' knuckles in Germany and my grandfather taught me how to make splendid homemade sausage. But only enough sausage to consume in two days should be made at a time. The Germans like to use equal parts of beef and veal and pork, but the meat cut off from six center-cut pork chops tastes better. The trick to sausage making is the sparing use of salt and the liberal use of real ground black pepper and ground sage and no other spice. Some chefs add mashed potato to fresh sausage meat. Big cakes of it baked or fried make a substantial meal.

Higher up the financial ladder come lamb chops and steak. You usually get what you pay for in meat. Top-quality lamb and beef is finished on grain, sometimes, in the case of beef, feeding one hundred and twenty days on corn. Kentucky oat-fed lamb has a marvelous flavor. Meat animals fed only on grass may have a yellowish fat of a different taste.

Steaks should be good to begin with. If the best is desired top-quality meat can be bought in bulk and stored by the butcher. A short loin might weigh fifty or sixty pounds and have considerable waste fat on it. Three of them are purchased. Most short loins need to be hung in the butcher's icebox for six weeks. While one is being eaten the others hang until they show the whiskers or mold which are a sign of well-hung meat. Steaks are cut as thin or thick as desired, always providing that too much fat is not cut away.

Pan-broiling a steak is perhaps the great American way. It means that the kitchen will be filled with dense greasy smoke. Something of iron, aluminum, or magnesium is heated red hot. Then a one-inch steak is burned two minutes on each side. Many Americans prefer that above any other method of cooking steak. Your Parisian chef would turn up his nose at such a procedure. He wants to know the exact minute that the meat course is to be served. Two hours before he may put the steak on a pipe shelf to gently warm it. Just so many minutes before dinner is announced the steak may be seared under blazing heat on both sides and promptly returned to the pipe shelf. Fifteen minutes before the course is to be served there may be additional cooking. Quite a ceremony it is, and the results are out of this world.

The tenderloin on a porterhouse disappears after about four steaks are cut off. The sirloin below that, when cut away from the bone, may be called a shell or Delmonico steak. With well-hung, good meat it can have a marvelous flavor and, if served individually, be about the best way to feed a hungry husband trying to lose weight. The shell steak should weigh one and a half pounds before cooking.

At the other end of the economic scale for steak come the choice or sirloin cuts wrapped in cellophane in a chain store. At the present buying power of money, a reasonable amount may buy a steak with fat in the center which can be cut at home into three adequate portions. If beautifully cooked, they are good. Roast beef is always better when the first three ribs can be purchased. Again, it is better to engage in long, slow cooking. It is a shame to let one fourth of the weight of expensive meat disintegrate in smoke. Club cuts of roast beef three quarters of an inch thick are carved for a stout husband. And on a blistering-hot summer morning, icy-cold roast beef may be the only thing that appeals to the appetite.

A double rib Frenched chop (there are four of these on a rack of lamb) with the backbone cut off and one rib cut completely out of the bottom might be expensive but two of them make a grand meal.

Practically all fresh fish is improved by a good sauce, and so is steak. But sauces made with salt and eggs and cream and flour are problems when treating obesity and allergy. If these are tolerated, in my humble opinion there is nothing to beat a perfectly prepared Béarnaise sauce. An electric blender can add to ease of preparation. There is no place where the American housewife falls down so hard as in the making of a good sauce. Dotting foods with butter is a poor substitute.

It wasn't only the snakes that St. Patrick drove out of

Ireland. One of the exports was a poor soggy potato called an Irish Cobbler. When an Irish Cobbler potato is rejected for destruction in a government surplus dump it may be sent to Florida, where all poor white potatoes go before they die. Almost as poor is something called a Katahdin. The hybridizers' dream of huge, disease-resistant potatoes of uniform shape, and the producers' sixfold increase in the use of fertilizer, have practically wrecked the potato business in Long Island and Maine.

No one wants a product that is devoid of flavor. But if you try you can still buy Prince Edward Island potatoes from Canada or Idaho or California potatoes. The growers in these three places still have some sense and depend upon good seed and good soil for flavor. Supposedly there is enough good potato land in Texas to feed the whole world all of the potatoes that could possibly be desired.

One of the culinary horrors perpetrated by restaurants in this country is called "french fries." To produce them it is necessary to have a large heated vat filled with stale hydrogenated oil. Even drained automobile crankcase oil is reprocessed before it is used again but not, apparently, the stuff used for french frying. Potatoes may be half cooked in the vat of fat and then stored in an icebox. When a customer comes in they may be taken out and doused again in the same oil. It is no wonder that they taste so badly.

To do a proper job the housewife needs a lot of gear. Electric french fryers which hold five pounds of fat, and with the correct temperature controls, are still a bit in the luxury class. A big iron special pot with a basket and a hooked rod can be bought. A pair of asbestos gloves hanging nearby on the wall isn't a bad idea, as a mistake made in regulating heat can start a fire. A real french frying thermometer is a good addition.

The fat should be beef dripping or melted suet or lard. This should be screened through a piece of gauze and a strainer after using. A square container is easier for storing it in the refrigerator and four or five times of using is enough. When the fat is at the correct temperature potatoes which have been chilled in the icebox for twenty-four hours are cut in half. It takes quite a bit of strength to force them through the crossed wires in a special french fry cutter. Then they are immersed in the hot fat. The basket is lifted out and hung on the hook until the thermometer again registers the correct reading. Then they are immersed again and tend to puff way up. It is quite a revelation as to how good potatoes can taste.

An old trick up along the Gaspé in Canada is to slice raw potatoes paper-thin. Then they are slowly cooked in butter or beef dripping in a covered pan, and have a delicious taste.

Don't make the mistake of trying to use up old boiled or baked white potatoes. Kept over, they undergo changes in flavor. Cook just enough so none are left over. Ordinary good fried white potatoes are made by slicing raw potatoes thin and boiling for ten minutes. The water is poured off and the potatoes are finished in whatever fat you like—salt butter, olive oil, beef or pork dripping (lamb dripping doesn't taste good), corn oil, olive oil, or lard. Beware of the synthetic fats. They can raise the devil in allergic people.

When slow weight reduction, with three things with a meal, is in order, one of the easiest ways to cook potatoes for breakfast is as follows: slice raw potatoes thin, cover them with water, and turn the heat to a level where the potatoes will have boiled approximately seventeen minutes by the time that the thirty-minute walk before breakfast is finished. Then the water is poured off. Sliced boiled potatoes with a bit of onion for flavor taste fine at breakfasttime.

Sweet potatoes are, or used to be before they started to dye them orange to look like yams, good food. When you are desperate about bringing up a fearfully allergic baby, resorting to the old Negro method of feeding babies nothing whatever but scraped cooked fat meat and mashed sweet potato and water and tea can work a small miracle.

If you know your way around in Virginia you can still buy what are called white sweet potatoes. They are dirty and ill formed and don't ship well. But, when cooked, they fairly drip sugar and have a wonderful taste. Be suspicious of sweet potatoes bought in the stores. Wash them at once in running water. If a yellow dye comes off take them back and demand your money. All of the yellow dyes can induce cancer in a susceptible individual.

For thorough enjoyment potatoes usually call for the good salt butter, which is the important dairy product. The ripening process which butter undergroes destroys much of the irritant inherent in milk and cream, and salt butter has splendid food value. But commercial butter has suffered from attack by the chemists. When slowly melted and poured into a thin glass container and stored in the icebox, it layers out into some weird-looking ingredients. Some of the trouble may be the blending of renovated butter with fresh in order to use up the old stored stuff. Whipped butter and sweet butter seem too much like milk to bother with.

Rice is an excellent form of starch. All forms—white, brown, instant, and cream of rice—seem to digest well. Cream-of-rice mush, if allowed to set in a thin layer in the icebox, and then cut into big squares and fried in butter has a delightfully delicate flavor. Reinforced with good butter and maple syrup, it is good enough to serve as a dessert. Wild rice is really a grass seed but it also seems to agree well.

Rice is rich in starch but low in protein and fat. Polishing rice gets rid of the vitamin B, which prevents beriberi. Valuable substances such as nitrogen and potash are also lost in polishing it. In China and Japan it is the custom to serve polished rice with soybean sauces, which supply the lacking elements. White rice or brown rice, if well cooked, are probably much better fare than is our treasured oatmeal. For some unknown reason living on oatmeal seems to promote dental caries and rickets. The worst teeth in the world may be seen in Scotland, where oatmeal is given high rank as a food. The bowlegs of a Scotsman may have the same origin.

The housewife needs to perfect her technique in preparing fried rice. Brown rice is cooked ahead of time. Then enough saffron and sliced stuffed olives and cooked mushrooms and parsley, or perhaps shaved and fried sweet peppers, are added to make an attractive dish, which is then fried in butter, dripping, olive oil, or corn oil. Children can be trained to like that every day, but it is not a substitute for fat meat.

Corn, in the form of hominy grits, or the big hominy called samp, or corn meal, can be substituted for potatoes or rice. The northern Italians often serve the corn meal mush they call polenta twice a day.

Of the spices, real ground black pepper and freshly ground paprika and saffron are outstanding. Paprika and saffron are high in vitamin content. It seems possible to use all of the spices freely with the exception of salt. Far too much salt is used by most of us. Some people even have the evil habit of adding salt to food before they taste it, which is, of course, an insult to the cook.

VEGETABLES

No one knows why the yellow vegetables seem better tolerated by children who have a background of eczema. Onions and beets and celery can sometimes be used with no apparent ill effect, but yellow vegetables always seem to be safer, perhaps because they aren't sprayed. (Farmers are beginning to spray carrots, however.) Waterless cooking is best for butternut squash and carrots. Young carrots cut in strips and cooked with a little syrup are a lot more appetizing than the soggy cross sections usually served. Everyone, I suppose, has some pet dislikes, and one of mine is the combination of peas and carrots served in cheap restaurants. Carrots and peas seem as inseparable as Abercrombie and Fitch.

Golden Cross bantam corn right out of the garden and served with plenty of butter is one of the taste treats in this world, and it is generally well tolerated. When the ears are a little past their prime, a thin knife blade can be run down each row and the milk of the corn squeezed out with a tablespoon. Extracting the milk from the corn is a messy job, but a good cook can do wonders with it. The canned yellow creamed corn is a good thing to have in the house, even if it contains a lot of husks and is diluted in various ways. It is perhaps the best of the canned vegetables. That old country dish of mashed turnip and potato, and butternut squash, and pumpkin for pie filling are all good.

Beans have never had a fair chance. The indigestible cellulose covering causes a lot of flatulence and general intestinal unhappiness. But beans have a high protein content and if some smart canner could just figure out a mechanical rather than a chemical method of getting the hide off them they should be a fine food. Long ago that was one of the grandmother's jobs in the household. She was expected to pop the lima beans for Saturday night supper. Dried lima beans were soaked in water until they swelled up. A slit was made in the skin and the bean squeezed out. After there were enough of them, and it took plenty, they were baked with a big square of home-cured salt pork. And a dinner for champions it made.

The best salad always seems to be alligator pear with a fine homemade french dressing. The trick in that seems to be to use six parts of real olive oil to one part of wine or tarragon vinegar and any other flavoring that is liked. Fresh celery with the strings removed and cut crosswise in quarter-inch slices and then served with a fine dressing is first rate. Lettuce is one of the hardest foods to digest that is known.

DESSERTS

Five raw fruits seem to cause too much irritation to bother with if there is allergy in the family. Raw oranges, apples, strawberries, tomatoes, and peaches can trouble lots of folks. Much safer are grapefruit, pears, bananas, grapes, and alligator pears. In season blueberries, raspberries, dead-ripe pineapple and melons, and plums can be agreeable. In a well-run home delicate fruits like raspberries and seedless grapes and blueberries can be spread out and every rotten one picked out. Then they are washed in a colander and left to dry in the air. After that they can be placed in the dish they are to be served in and put in the icebox to chill. You don't see those fruits served cool and clean and dry in a restaurant. Bananas which have never been frozen should be kept at room temperature until freckled. Pears should also be ripened in a dark warm room.

One embittered soul figured out that only one in six hundred of the honeydew melons and canteloupe that flood into New York City in season will ever be fit to eat. A ripe melon at full flavor should tumble off a green vine. Picked more than six days before maturity, they never reach perfection. Probably most of them are picked twelve to fourteen days before they are ripe. The middle of the side, not the end, should press in and stay in like a ripe apple and a fine perfume should be noticeable.

No one knows why grapefruit are so much better tolerated than oranges. Chemically there is some difference. Canned juices and frozen juices are not allowed. They usually have a poor taste unless oil from the skin is added, and that can be quite irritating.

You could journey from New York to Florida, stopping at restaurants along the way, and never find grapefruit properly prepared. That takes a minute of extra time. The membrane between the cells is indigestible, so each partition should be cut around inside with a thin sharp knife and the seeds, if any, removed. When you get through eating such a grapefruit portion a perfect framework remains. Grapefruit and grapes are a great cross to the managers of private and public restaurants, since there seems to be no way of serving them any way but ripe. But pears and bananas and melons and alligator pears and pineapple can all be served as green as grass, then nothing is lost by getting overripe. The fact that they are uneatable never seems to occur to the restaurateur. Such fruits are almost as bad as the sliced green tomatoes faintly tinged with pink that are served with steak. Ripe fruit is hard to get. But all of the canned fruits seem usually to be well tolerated. The juice of canned fruit can be taken, but not canned fruit juice. Home-canned fruits taste better than the kind in the stores. Reinforcing them with the juice of one half of a fresh grapefruit, or a cut-up freckled banana, or peeled and seeded grapes, can add to the enjoyment of eating them.

One of the safest foods in the tropics is canned fruit. The natives may have been immunized over the centuries to the local infections, but when strangers go there they are fair game. Even cleaning teeth with tap water and toothpaste can start the forty bowel movements a day. Toothpaste cannot be trusted to sterilize water. If you must travel in the tropics depend largely on weak alcohol and heat and sugar to kill off the bad infections.

Weak alcohol, which the French call *vin de l'eau*, is a splendid disinfectant. A good rule in the tropics is never to drink plain unboiled water, even if especially bottled. The label may be wrong. One quarter of a glass of wine and three quarters of a glass of water usually is a safe drink if allowed to stand a few minutes. Bottled beer is also a safe beverage. In some of the tropical countries local superstition has it that washing dishes in hot water causes rheumatism in the hands, so dishes are washed in cold water. As a result dishes may be infected. Hot foods and canned fruit are usually safest when you are near the equator. Strong sugar solutions used to preserve fruit seem to discourage virulent bacteria.

The housewife should use sugar for the preparation of fruit compote or canned fruit, and if any of her children are underweight it can be added to raw fruit and rice. But on the whole the use of sugar should be discouraged. It is a very concentrated carbohydrate and in the form of commercial candy can apparently increase cavities in soft teeth at a tremendous rate. Many children need to eat five or six times a day and natural sugars like ripe bananas and dates and figs and seedless raisins are excellent tidbits to have on hand. Maple syrup is a good thing to serve with corn cakes and yeast-risen buckwheat cakes. Jams and jellies are healthy foods, as is honey.

Desserts other than canned and raw fruit pose a problem for many allergic families. The children may get some pleasure and value out of puddings and pie fillings, but cake and cookies should be kept out of the picture, which is too bad. When a woman is full of pent-up nervous energy nothing seems to relieve her quite so much as making a batch of what are called "brownies," and they can raise the very devil if any of her children have skin trouble or soft teeth.

Cooking milk and eggs twenty-two minutes seems to destroy the qualities that irritate many people. Rice pudding with raisins and tapioca pudding require baking longer than that and are good healthy desserts. A passable pie crust which will not roll but can be patched together can be made by an artistic cook out of potato flour and ice water and sugar and butter. That is only for the bottom crust, where it can be easily forgotten. It might be a good thing for the country if the top crusts on pies were all eliminated. If people could get the idea that the top crust is fattening it would be an advance. Not that top or bottom makes any difference, of course, but it is easier to abandon the bottom crust. Only the filling is important. Butternut squash, pumpkin, mince, apple, plum, and peach pie filling can be wonderful culinary adventures. But, owing to the commercial bakeries, good pie made without chemicals is fast disappearing from the American cuisine, and that is too bad. An easy fortune awaits anyone who can restore good pie with no top crust to New York City.

Coffee and tea when well made are good beverages. Don't use furiously boiling water when making coffee by the drip method. The temperature of the water should be just below boiling, otherwise an irritating substance called mercaptan will be extracted. In parts of the country there are so many degrees of hardness in the water that it is impossible to make good tea or coffee, in which case distilled water should be used. Many people over the age of sixty-five should not expect to fall asleep readily for hours after drinking a cup of tea or coffee, so they may have to dispense with it for the evening meal. There seems to be little advantage to extracting part of the caffeine in special preparations of coffee. It is more sensible to take smaller portions of the real thing.

I must be careful. Talk about food can get out of hand.

The first thing I know, this may degenerate into one more cookbook, which is far from my desire. I just want to emphasize that the housewife, with her power of the purse and her way of preparing her purchases, controls our destiny.

It seems probable that the eternal economic plight of our farmers has a simple explanation. They are raising the wrong things. Little of the grain and milk and chicken and eggs and vegetables raised today can be classed as needed. What Americans want is beef and lamb and veal and pork.

Two acres of grassland on a hilly New England farm will furnish the same energy for a steer as one hundred and sixty acres of pasture land in certain areas of the West. And, again, all flesh is grass.

Private capital could take over a whole county in New England for use as a pilot plant. You wouldn't want the clammy hand of government mixed up in it except for inspection. With a processing plant and a collecting system, every farmer in the county could be put to work raising animals. Farmers need a cash crop, but with proper planning that could be arranged.

With most of them going forward to animal husbandry, we could relegate plows to the Smithsonian. The plow is the main cause of muddy streams and rivers in the springtime. And a muddy stream means that we are dissipating our greatest natural resource—our topsoil.

Postscript

Reading over this manuscript has made me realize that my dear wife is right, as usual. When the writing has been a bit on the dull side it is because I have been too weary. For I can assure you that there is nothing dull about the practice of medicine.

It may seem that I am too proud of my patients. Well! I am proud of them. They are wonderful people, who fight when it is carefully explained to them what they are fighting for. And that I like.

There aren't too many things in this life that you can be sure of, but of this I feel certain: this may well be my first and last venture into the realm of literature.

Like a little colored boy I took care of once in an army hospital in France. He had been caught in a barrage of mustard gas and had to run for his life. When completely exhausted he sat down on ground that had been drenched with mustard. That burned a hole through the seat of his pants. It was an honorable wound, but nothing he could brag about to the folks back home. *Convalescent sergeants and corporals sitting around the ward with nothing to do would take pleasure in worrying little Willy Bell. One day one of them asked him what he was going to do in the next war. Suspiciously Willy Bell asked, "What do you mean, the next war?"*

"Oh, there is always a next war, Willy," the corporal airily replied.

Quoth Willy, "Lemme tell you sump'in, Corporal. If there's any next war, why, I live in a house in a piece of woods down in Georgia. And they're going to have to burn the house and burn the woods and sift the ashes to get me."

While I have been off on this long ramble through the fields of medicine winter and spring have gone and now it is summertime. At last I feel free to take my boat out. The cares of the day vanish with the first savage strike of a bluefish in the tide rip. Hooking one knee over the tiller of the little Sheilah, I can head toward home while filleting a couple of fish for dinner.

And with the sun going down, life is good.

INDEX

Abscess, 166
Acidosis, 40
Acne, 139, 146, 181, 210
Active acetate, 56
Adrenalin, 152
Afrika Korps, 36
Air conditioning, 157
Albumin, 113–14
Alcohol, 164, 166, 175, 180, 195, 196, 209–10; in anti-obesity routine, 71, 104, 122–23
Alcoholic neuritis, 180
Allergic cerebellar angiospasm, 187, 189
Allergic stupor, 146, 148, 187, 189
Allergic stupor, 146, 148
Allergy, 6, 133–44, 145–54
Altered reaction, 135
American Museum of Natural History, 33
Amino acids, 37, 43, 74, 78, 105, 111, 130, 191, 192, 204, 205–6
Anaphylaxis, 135
Andersen, Karsten, 38–39
Antibiotics, 158
Anticoagulants, 73
Anti-obesity routine, 35–44
Antra, 167–70
Antritis. See Sinus trouble
Anxiety state, 123, 125–26
Appendicitis, 139, 177

Apprehension, feeling of, 121
Army of Occupation, 28
Arsenic poisoning, 212
Arterial hypertension, 122
Arteries, hardening of. See Hardening of the arteries
Arteriosclerosis, 2, 105, 107, 110, 112, 113, 116
Arthritis. See Osteoarthritis; Rheumatoid arthritis; Villous arthritis
Arthus' phenomenon, 152
Aspirin, 104, 110, 159, 176
Asthma, 18, 137, 139, 141, 142, 153, 210
Atheroma, 110
Athlete's foot, 108, 146, 181–85
Atopy, 135
Auricular flutter, 181

Back joints, exercise for arthritic, 90–97, 104, 110–11, 123, 149
Bacterial allergy, 140, 149, 155–65
Bailey, Cameron V., 51–52
Baldness, 51
Base Hospital No. Eight, 21
Beef stew, 22–23
Bellevue Hospital, 18, 24, 38
Bell's palsy, 140
Beriberi, 229
"Big bad seven," the, 166, 206–9
Bile, 127, 131, 150

CPSIA information can be obtained
at www.ICGtesting.com
Printed in the USA
BVHW04s0515090418
512462BV00009B/233/P

9 781258 440961